Raising Emotionally Healthy Children In Today's Society

Helpful Tips Since They Did Not Come With An Instruction Manual

Maria Reis, MA

The content contained within this book may not be reproduced, duplicated, or transmitted without direct written permission from the author or the publisher.

Under no circumstances will any blame or legal responsibility be held against the publisher, or author, for any damages, reparation, or monetary loss due to the information contained within this book, either directly or indirectly.

Legal Notice:

This book is copyright-protected. It is only for personal use. You cannot amend, distribute, sell, use, quote, or paraphrase any part or the content within this book without the consent of the author or publisher.

Disclaimer Notice:

Please note the information contained within this document is for educational and entertainment purposes only. All efforts have been executed to present accurate, up-to-date, reliable, and complete information. No warranties of any kind are declared or implied. Readers acknowledge that the author is not engaged in rendering legal, financial, medical, or professional advice. The content within this book has been derived from various sources. Please consult a licensed professional before attempting any techniques outlined in this book.

By reading this document, the reader agrees that under no circumstances is the author responsible for any direct or indirect losses incurred as a result of the use of the information contained within this document, including, but not limited to, errors, omissions, or inaccuracies.

Copyright © 2023 by Maria Reis, MA

All rights reserved.

No portion of this book may be reproduced without written permission from the publisher or author, except as permitted by U.S. copyright law.

Contents

Introduction		1
1.	Chapter 1: Determining What Type of Parent You Are	4
2.	Chapter 2: What's the Best Approach to Use for My Child?	23
3.	Chapter 3: A Healthy Expression of Emotions	36
4.	Chapter 4: Praise and Encouragement	52
5.	Chapter 5: Teaching Social Intelligence	64
6.	Chapter 6: Positive Role Modeling	75
7.	Chapter 7: Conflict Resolution	87
8.	Chapter 8: Helping Your Child Overcome Obstacles in Life	97
9.	Chapter 9: Fostering Independence and Responsibility	106
10.	Chapter 10: Navigating the Digital Age Consciously	116
Bonus: Cultivating Emotional Intelligence as a Family		124
Conclusion		134
References		144

Introduction

Sitting across from Angela, I could see the weariness in her eyes as she rubbed her temples. "I just don't know how to get through to Sophia lately," she sighed. "It's like she's become a whole different child since she started middle school. I feel like everything sets her off and any little comment turns into World War III around here!" Angela was depleted, desperate to reconnect with the daughter she once knew. She could hardly remember the last relaxed, fun interaction with her. Although Sophia was home, Angela agonized over the emotional distance stretching between them.

I nodded with empathy, having fielded numerous calls over the years from confused parents whose children had become strangers. "The early teen years can be tough as they figure themselves out," I acknowledged. "But there are always strategies we can use to try to stay connected." Even behind eye rolls and one-word answers, opportunities exist to rediscover the children we still know and love. It's easy to lose heart when previous tactics of engagement stop working. Yet if we release the familiar approaches that once worked and listen patiently for clues to what they now crave, breakthroughs happen.

In my many years as a family counselor, I've learned that children's acting out is often a plea for connection. When children feel truly seen, heard, and understood—that their needs and emotions matter—tension dissipates. Attuning at that level requires moving past our triggers into an open-hearted presence. Listening without judgment, refraining from unsolicited advice, focusing wholeheartedly on understanding—this demonstrates that their inner world matters and paves the way for vulnerable sharing. Children often test our unconditional commitment before trusting us with their tenderest struggles. Staying unruffled signals the depth of caring they seek.

I'll never forget Emily, who came to me at her wit's end with 7-year-old Leo. His defiant meltdowns exhausted them both. As we talked, I learned that Leo struggled to process his big feelings, lacking the words to express how upset he felt. When emotions overwhelmed him, his behavior unraveled. I coached Emily to name Leo's emotions in real time, acknowledging rather than dismissing the feelings beneath the behavior. We brainstormed healthy outlets so these intense feelings wouldn't erupt but could be channeled. It wasn't overnight magic, but they broke through. Leo's now thriving, and Emily's confidence as a parent has soared. Whenever she panicked, I reminded Emily to see Leo's heart beneath the behavior. She just needed support accessing her own patience and creativity again.

There's no formula guaranteed to work with every child every time. But over years of studying families, small yet mighty tools emerged that can guide beyond power struggles and into partnership. Little things that say, "I see you. I hear you. You matter." The pages ahead share these gems gathered from tireless work alongside caregivers and children of all ages and temperaments. You'll discover how to forge meaningful connections, even amidst the messiness. I'll equip you to respond to outbursts with empathy versus escalation and to nurture cooperation and accountability. Together, we'll build your confidence and trust.

My hope is to walk with you beyond "perfect parenting" clichés. If you're willing to progress with a spirit of curiosity and courage, together, we might build compassionate havens where your children can thrive. What do you need right now—a listening ear? Fresh ideas? Or perhaps just the encouragement that this too shall pass? I'm here to offer support each step of the way. You don't have to figure this out alone. I've been in your shoes and have seen many find their footing again. Lean on me as your partner and sounding board.

I know the exhaustion seeping into your bones some days when defusing another argument seems impossible. I've shed those same tears, unsure if your child will ever share their secret struggles, wondering if the walls between you might permanently harden. But there is always light glinting somewhere in darkness if we adjust our gaze. Together, let's rediscover the tools and tenacity required to illuminate the way.

Chapter One

Chapter 1: Determining What Type of Parent You Are

Most of us grow up telling ourselves that when we become parents, "I am going to be different than my parents were with me. I will do things differently." Yet despite our best intentions, many of us end up adopting similar approaches as our own parents. Why does this happen?

In this chapter, we'll explore the main parenting styles—authoritative, authoritarian, permissive, and uninvolved—including the behaviors and attitudes that characterize each one. Examining these parenting types can shed light on our innate tendencies and show us where we may be staying stuck in generational patterns versus nurturing our children's unique needs.

I'll guide you through a series of reflective questions to identify your current parenting style and tendencies: How do you communicate with your child? How do you handle rule-setting and discipline? How engaged and responsive are you on a day-to-day basis? As you tally up the results objectively, you may find you align strongly with one style or a mix of approaches.

Gaining this clarity is so important before we dive into practical techniques for emotionally connecting with children because our overall style sets the tone for how receptive our children will be to any given strategy we try. If we are clingy or punitive rather than consistent and caring, that colors how they receive our efforts to guide them.

The goal here is not to judge wherever you land on the parenting style spectrum. Rather, it's to cultivate honest awareness so you can determine if this aligns with the type of caregiver you aspire to be for your unique child. Does your current approach offer a nurturing space that is secure for your young one to thrive and flourish? If not, the upcoming chapters will expand your toolkit to better support their growth with flexibility and understanding.

Parenting Styles

Parenting styles generally fall into four primary categories: authoritative, authoritarian, permissive, and uninvolved. While no parent adheres rigidly to any one style, recognizing your innate tendencies can help you play to your strengths and fill any gaps in meeting your child's needs. Let's explore the key traits of each so you can evaluate your own approach objectively.

Authoritative Parents

Authoritative parents balance nurture and structure, responding warmly while maintaining reasonable expectations. They actively listen to their children's thoughts and feelings, encouraging independence through two-way communication. Children of authoritative parents tend to be self-assured, resilient, and socially responsible. These parents offer guidance, provide rationale for rules, and reinforce positive behaviors. Their children feel heard and respected, developing internal motivation and learning to self-regulate behavior. Authoritative caregivers adapt to the different needs of individual children while upholding developmentally appropriate responsibilities.

For example, when Lisa's seven-year-old son forgot his homework, she asked him open-ended questions to understand why and problem-solved so he'd develop strategies to remember next time. She expressed empathy and firm optimism in his ability to get organized. Lisa resisted scolding or shaming him for this mistake, instead exploring factors that led him to forget. She validated that it's hard to stay on top of things at the end of a long school day. Together, they discussed using a planner and packing his bag the night before to set him up for success.

Children of authoritative parents tend to thrive, developing independence, self-confidence, and strong coping abilities as they grow older. With responsive support, rational limits, and open communication from a young age, they internalize self-discipline and decision-making skills. Though not perfect, these children can acknowledge and learn from mistakes with their sense of worth intact. Having cultivated emotional intelligence through parental attunement, they can healthily self-soothe and communicate their needs. With autonomy balanced by accountability, authoritative parenting produces resilient, community-minded adults. Children nurtured in this way have absorbed problem-solving abilities from collaborative discipline and negotiations.

While authoritative parents aim for balance, they may forget to consistently temper discipline with warmth. In trying to build independence, they might overestimate a young child's capacity to self-manage when providing abundant choices early on. Their children's relative comfort with speaking up can mask issues related to lacking grit when challenges arise.

Tips for authoritative parents include tracking their own follow-through on stated limits and agreed-upon consequences. Checking in with teachers can reveal if more parental focus on compliance and maturity is needed currently. Allowing children to complete difficult chores without jumping in to help builds self-reliance.

Authoritarian Parents

Authoritarian caregivers adhere to rigid discipline with strict expectations for obedience. They consult themselves rather than tuning into the child's perspective. While their objective is control and conformity, children often internally rebel and become anxious or defiant. These parents rely on negative reinforcement, like shaming and threats, instead of constructive feedback. They offer directives rather than explanations when enforcing rules. Authoritarian parents often neglect to nurture emotional skills as they focus narrowly on compliant behavior.

John demands that his son complete an hour of math worksheets every night. When the child objects, John threatens to ground him. He mandates obedience to his rules rather than listening to his son's perspective or trying to grasp underlying challenges. John dismisses his son's feedback that the work is repetitive and boring. He refuses to acknowledge the emotional withdrawal and lack of intrinsic motivation created by his rigid approach. John reminds his son that his role is to comply without complaint.

Children raised by authoritarian parents often struggle with anxiety, diminished self-esteem, and difficulty trusting their own judgment. The rigid control and harsh critique during formative years hinder emotional security and executive functioning. Focused on obeying strict rules, they have less opportunity to make choices and learn from natural consequences. Their perfectionism and resentment can crystallize into defiance or disconnection. The external pressure to comply makes them doubt their inner wisdom. Quick to self-blame but lacking self-efficacy, they react to challenges with helpless resignation. Some authoritarian-parented adults rigidly cling to rules for security, while others reject all boundaries.

Authoritarian parents often struggle to recognize when their forceful, disciplinarian approach causes children to shut down or actively rebel. Strict rule enforcement sometimes lacks an explanation of the reasoning behind those rules. This style can also lead to difficulty empathizing with the child's perspective when correcting behavior, focusing exclusively on compliance. Checks for understanding the impacts on a child's emotional state rarely occur.

Useful feedback tips include taking time to solicit the child's viewpoint before reacting to misbehavior. Even while upholding standards, clarify the purpose of rules and allow some discussion. Additionally, making notes when teachers describe withdrawn moods or intense reactions from the child at school provides insight into authoritarian parenting consequences.

Permissive Parents

Permissive parents behave more like a friend than an authority figure. They make few demands and give considerable self-governance to children, intervening only as a last resort. These well-intended caregivers seek to foster high self-esteem through "conditional love" based on children's happiness rather than responsibility. Permissive parents avoid confrontation by accommodating their children's preferences. They rely on gentle persuasion and offer bribes to get children to cooperate. This overly lenient approach fails to provide needed structure and accountability.

Julie asks her daughter's permission before signing her up for activities. She avoids enforcing homework time because it leads to too much whining and frustration. Julie caves to her daughter's desires for the path of least resistance. Julie struggles to set any structure or expectations, finding it easier to let her daughter dictate the schedule. She foregoes rules about technology usage or bedtimes to avoid being the "bad cop." Over time, Julie feels increasingly unable to place limits as her daughter grows more entitled.

Children of permissive parents may initially seem happiest with few demands and abundant freedom. But lacking structure, these children often feel insecure and act entitled or aimless when older. They expect others to meet their needs without recognizing their own responsibility. Never having developed grit through incremental challenges or logical incentives, they may quit easily with poor self-regulation skills. Permissive parenting often produces greatly disappointed young adults still hoping to be rescued from self-created predicaments. Unprepared for independent functioning, they postpone adult milestones and resent those who try to hold them accountable. Some do ultimately find their way after painfully learning life lessons on their own.

Permissive parents often assume children naturally develop the ability to self-moderate behavior without guidance, failing to see the instability this lack of boundaries creates. They may genuinely believe granting considerable autonomy shows care, forgetting that consistent structure helps children feel safe as well. By sheltering children from experiencing struggles, they undermine grit and personal responsibility.

Useful input includes noticing if children still seek parental guidance and reassurance, which indicates that their maturity level requires more involved support. Asking teachers to assess organizational skills, self-control, and work completion illuminates capabilities to direct one's own learning. Reflecting on what level of oversight is developmentally appropriate for their child's current age would also help permissive parents gain perspective.

Uninvolved Parents

Uninvolved parents offer little time, communication, nurturing, or structure. Some are unable due to circumstances, while others are apathetic to the duties of child-rearing. With few checks on behavior combined with emotional neglect, these children often lack self-regulation and decision-making abilities. Uninvolved parents are detached in interactions with children and minimize responding to bids for attention. Consumed with their own needs first, these caregivers rarely monitor schoolwork, friendships, or general well-being.

Though Peggy is physically present with her children, she is emotionally unavailable and distracted by her phone and computer. Her children try unsuccessfully to get her attention as she zones out, completely disengaged. They've learned the ineffectiveness of turning to her for guidance. Peggy's children experience her as detached even in moments of connection, struggling to share their feelings or provide reassurance. Her inattention leaves them insecure, trying desperately to please or provoke reactions.

With little affection, attention, or reliable guidance from parents, these children tend to lack confidence and decision-making abilities. Often left to their own devices, they feel insecure in relationships and school with no one monitoring their progress or well-being. Growing up, they may crave love through unhealthy dependencies or rebel against authority figures. Their emotional and social maturity tends to lag behind their peers. Sadly, the detached dynamic with uninvolved parents often persists throughout adulthood, with minimal contact or depth of connection. Alternatively, some who felt invisible to their parents seek validation obsessively in vain attempts to heal these attachment wounds.

Uninvolved parents struggle to recognize their lack of awareness of major events, responsibilities, and milestones in their child's daily life. Unless informed by others, they often fail to attune to the child's shifting interests over time. The lack of engagement around emotional needs also takes a cumulative toll that goes unseen.

Tips here involve adding school dates, extracurricular activities, and social commitments to digital calendars and setting notifications to remember. Regularly asking children open-ended questions about friendships, hobbies, worries, and goals builds connectivity. Teachers can share specifics around talents and challenges that shape supportive involvement.

Now that you have an overview, take some time to reflect on your own inclinations. Do you skew toward authority or leniency? Engaged or hands-off? Getting clear on your natural style allows you to play to those tendencies while balancing where needed. No parent is perfect, but awareness of your type aids in playing to your strengths.

What Type of Parent Are You?

Before diving into practical strategies for connecting with and disciplining children, it's vital we start by looking in the mirror. Every parent brings innate tendencies into their caregiving—some stemming from how we were parented and others tied to our personality. Left unexamined, these reflexive patterns often run on autopilot, even when unproductive or unhealthy.

This section provides an opportunity to shine some light on your unique parenting instincts. We will explore four common styles—permissive, authoritative, authoritarian, and uninvolved—including the typical behaviors and attitudes behind each approach. As you reflect honestly on your reactions across typical scenarios, you will likely see aspects of yourself aligning with several styles depending on the circumstance or child. Very few parents exhibit pure archetypes.

Gaining this insight empowers you to leverage your strengths while identifying areas for growth. Perhaps you excel at emotional attunement but need help upholding structure. Maybe you default to strictness when increased empathy and listening would better motivate. Rather than judge where you fall short, use this knowledge to expand your range and cultivate versatility. Children don't come with manuals, nor are our own upbringings flawless templates. We are all learning as we go.

Use this exploration to get curious, not critical, regarding your parenting instincts. Instead of solidifying your identity as one kind of caregiver, discover the diversity of tools you can utilize. Compassion for ourselves allows compassion for our children as we parent with intention rather than habit. Let's reflect on where you shine as well as any blind spots so you can be the nurturing guide your child needs as they grow.

Communication Approach

Do you actively solicit your child's perspective before making decisions? Are you open to feedback or more directive in your manner? Assess whether you are responsive or if you ignore bids for attention. Tuning in to your children's input, listening fully without judgment, and providing empathy advances their emotional intelligence. Children behave better when respected, taken seriously, and treated as capable communicators. Make sure exchanges feel two-way rather than top-down lectures.

Expectations and Boundaries

Determine whether you have clearly articulated rules and responsibilities. Do you enforce these consistently or only intermittently? Evaluate whether your expectations match your child's developmental abilities. Research shows that consistent limits reinforce security even when testing them. Clearly defined expectations must adapt over time as new freedoms and duties align with growing maturity. Ensure that you're not overwhelming children's capacities while still providing needed structure.

Discipline Style

When rules are broken, or values are violated, do you use empathetic communication and natural consequences, or do you default to anger and punishment? Reflect on whether discipline feels collaborative or combative. Children are neurobiologically primed to resist authoritarian tactics, which corrode the psychological safety needed for behavioral change. Compassionate correction aligned with values evokes cooperation, not rebellion. Make discipline an opportunity for emotional and ethical learning.

Involvement Level

How attuned are you to your child's friendships, interests, school progress, and general well-being? Can you actively recall recent details, or are you more removed from their daily lives? Presence and attunement should increase as children age, with supervision easing only gradually. Disconnection deprives children of guidance in navigating complex academic pressures, peer issues, and identity development milestones. Stay engaged to spot problems early and provide essential support.

Taking an honest inventory of these dynamics can reveal whether you skew authoritative, authoritarian, permissive, or disengaged. Online parenting quizzes provide ratings across these measures after answering a survey about your reactions to common scenarios. Comparing your experienced parenting reality to these best practice types can illuminate areas for improvement.

Keep in mind that few parents fit neatly into a single style. Most of us fluctuate based on circumstances, stress levels, and our children's changing developmental stages. With self-awareness, we can play to our inherent strengths while compensating where needed. Recognizing your tendencies is a vital first step to evolving positively.

Parenting Style Quiz

This quiz will assist in determining which style you lean toward. For each question, choose the response that best reflects your typical reactions and approach.

You notice your child struggling socially. You:

A) tell them to toughen up and figure it out themselves

B) role-play situations to expand their skills

C) intervene directly with their friends to solve their problems

D) feel unsure how to help effectively

Your child gets a poor grade. You:

A) punish them by taking away privileges

B) have a conversation about improving study habits

C) assume the work is too hard and don't want them to feel bad

D) aren't aware because you don't monitor their grades

Your child wants to quit sports. You:

A) refuse and demand they finish the season

B) explore reasons and have an open dialogue about options

C) allow them to quit despite long-term commitments

D) let them decide without your input

Your child gets a bad grade on a test after neglecting to study. You:

A) ground them from activities until grades improve

B) help them come up with a study schedule for next time

C) assume the material was too advanced and don't want them to feel inadequate

D) don't really follow up on their academic progress

Your child wants highlights in their hair, which you believe is inappropriate. You:

A) refuse to allow it—your rules are not up for discussion

B) have an open talk about why you feel highlights aren't suitable

C) agree immediately so your child can express individuality

D) stay silent with indifference

Your child wants to enroll in dance classes that conflict with family dinnertime. You:

A) decline to exchange family time for an activity you didn't preapprove

B) Weigh the pros/cons of adjusting the dinner routine to accommodate their interest

C) instantly change your usual dinner plans so they can participate

D) leave the decision entirely up to your child

Your child gets frustrated trying to build a complex Lego structure. You:

A) tell them that no one will help them in life if they can't problem-solve alone

B) offer reassuring guidance and collaborate to support their efforts

C) take over building it yourself so they don't have negative emotions

D) are preoccupied and unaware of their difficulty

Your child prefers to play video games after school rather than do homework. You:

A) ban all video games until homework is done each day

B) help them schedule homework first, then agree upon an appropriate amount of gaming time

C) let them play as long as they want to avoid nagging about homework

D) assume that homework gets done without checking

Your child wants to wear non-weather-appropriate clothes to school. You:

A) prohibit them from wearing the wrong seasonal attire

B) provide choices between appropriate outfit alternatives

C) allow them to wear whatever they choose to express themselves

D) don't notice what they wear out the door

Your child wants to quit the travel soccer team mid-season. You:
A) refuse to let them quit once commitments are made
B) discuss reasons and explore potentially reasonable solutions
C) immediately allow them to follow their changing interests
D) take a hands-off approach regarding their activities

Scoring & Interpretation:

Mostly As = Authoritarian leanings

Mostly Bs = Authoritative tendencies

Mostly Cs = Permissive inclinations

Mostly Ds = Uninvolved style

No parent aligns perfectly with one single style. See this assessment as a starting point to build awareness rather than definitive labeling. Continue observing your reactions in real-time and notice when increased nurture, structure, or guidance is needed. Leverage your strengths while developing versatility to evolve across your child's emerging needs.

It's a

Journey

The journey of raising children is filled with questions, doubts, and continual decision points. We won't handle every situation perfectly; there is no such thing as a "perfect parent." But striving to show up open-hearted, as present as possible with the knowledge we have, matters immensely.

This chapter aimed to shed light on innate tendencies you may not have recognized in yourself before as a caregiver. Identifying your natural inclinations empowers you. Now you can play to your strengths confidently while noting areas for growth. Perhaps you excel at nurture but need support on structure, or vice versa. Leveraging self-awareness is the key.

Keep in mind that no parent fits neatly into a static box. Our children grow and change across developmental stages, needing different approaches as they mature. We, too, can evolve our skills, becoming increasingly attentive and responsive to each child's needs. Use this knowledge as a compass guiding you, not as a label defining limitations on who you can become for the young people relying on you.

Progress, not perfection, is what allows us all to become the safe havens our children need. Despite missteps, keep striving to hear them, see them, and understand them. It is through the patient work of attuning that trust builds. With trust comes opportunities to impart life's lessons while sending an unshakable message: You matter. Our relationship matters. Let's move forward together.

Case Study: Struggling with Authoritarian Parenting

Sarah is a 42-year-old mother of three children: Emma (age 15), Aiden (age 12), and Zoe (age 8). As Sarah reflects on her parenting style after reading this chapter, she realizes that she skews toward an authoritarian approach.

Like the vignette in the chapter, Sarah often demands obedience from her children without much open communication. For example, she imposed a rule that they must complete 30 minutes of math worksheets per night, similar to John in the example. Her intention is to ensure that they are academically successful, but her rigid style has led to mixed results.

Emma has always been defiant in response to Sarah's authoritarian parenting. She rebels against most rules and engages in lying and sneaking out without permission. Recently, Emma has started failing classes and skipping school, causing huge arguments at home. Sarah grounds Emma frequently but hasn't been able to get through to her.

In contrast, Aiden complies with Sarah's rules to avoid conflict. However, his demeanor is often anxious and withdrawn around Sarah. At parent/teacher conferences, Sarah was shocked to learn that Aiden suffers from low self-confidence and perfectionistic tendencies despite good grades. The counselor explained that this can reflect authoritarian parenting dynamics.

Zoe still aims to please overall as the youngest child. But Sarah sees signs that Zoe may take the route of anxiety and compliance like Aiden versus outright rebellion like Emma. Zoe worries about getting in trouble and lacks decisiveness, looking to Sarah for direction.

Through reading about parenting styles, Sarah recognizes that she needs more balance, nurture, and empathy alongside structure and discipline. She now sees the consequences of her rigid approach—defiance in one child, anxiety in another, and emerging insecurity in the youngest.

Sarah reflects deeper on her own upbringing, recalling that her father was critical and demanding, just as she is with her children. She determines not to let her generational patterns continue to harmfully impact her children's self-esteem and emotional health.

First, Sarah plans to stop using humiliation, like calling children "lazy" or "irresponsible" when they struggle with schoolwork. She will replace shaming with collaborative problem-solving focused on the behavior, not attacking their character.

Second, Sarah will create reasonable rules with her children's input, allowing some negotiating to build buy-in. She will explain her rationale for needing balance and planning ahead.

Third, Sarah commits to designing fair, proportional consequences so that discipline feels humane, not vindictive or random. She will focus any corrective talks on values, not condemnation, and empathy, not attacks.

Finally, Sarah will carve out regular one-on-one time with each child—no agenda except emotional check-ins and listening. She wants them to feel truly seen and cared about, not just judged for rule-following.

With authoritarianism deeply entrenched over the years, Sarah expects setbacks where old habits resurface as she implements changes. However, she is determined to keep evolving her parenting, even attending counseling herself. She refuses to remain rigidly stuck even if the deviation from familiar control elicits short-term power struggles. Sarah commits wholeheartedly to fostering the security and self-efficacy her children deserve.

Case Study: Moving from Permissive to Authoritative Parenting

Juanita is a 38-year-old single mother to a daughter, Gabby, age nine. Having grown up with authoritarian parents herself, Juanita strived to give Gabby abundant freedom and nurture as a child. However, Gabby has become quite entitled and defiant as she nears the preteen years.

Like Julie's situation described in the permissive parents section, Juanita avoids enforcing bedtimes, rules around technology usage, or even timely schoolwork completion. She struggles to confront Gabby's whining and tantrums when she requests cooperation. Juanita tends to instantly cave to her daughter's demands, whether it's buying expensive items mid-grocery trip or letting Gabby skip soccer practice to go out for ice cream instead.

At recent parent/teacher conferences, Gabby's fourth-grade teacher raised concerns about her lagging math skills, incomplete homework, and distracting classroom chatter. Juanita realized with shock that Gabby was struggling significantly—news missed without proper oversight of schoolwork and assessments at home. Gabby's teacher also noted that Gabby often expects special exceptions from agreed-upon class rules and acts entitled with her peers.

Juanita recognizes from the chapter that her permissive, child-centered parenting style has prevented Gabby from building essential life skills like organization, grit, and responsible decision-making. While Juanita succeeded in making Gabby feel cherished, she now sees the cost of lax structure and accountability. Gabby seems ill-prepared to handle routine frustrations or work hard toward goals that require perseverance but provide delayed gratification.

As Juanita reflects on her upbringing dominated by rigid authoritarianism, she understands the roots of her extreme leniency and rescuing. But Juanita now commits to finding balance as an authoritative parent instead. First, she will create House Rules with Gabby's input—defining bedtime, technology guidelines, homework expectations, and contributions to chores. She will post this as a visual reminder, upholding consistency even when Gabby initially complains about increased structure.

Second, Juanita pledges to hold unruffled boundaries, empathetically acknowledging Gabby's feelings without relinquishing reasonable limits or exceptions. She will help Gabby build distress tolerance and adapt to the structure. Juanita will offer Gabby a sense of control via limited choices within boundaries.

Finally, Juanita will schedule weekly check-ins regarding Gabby's progress and pitfalls related to the new House Rules. They will collaboratively problem-solve any adjustments needed, keeping communication open about how increased responsibilities feel for Gabby. Juanita will lean into curiosity, not judgment, seeking to guide Gabby as she learns self-management.

Juanita feels nervous yet hopeful about establishing herself as an authoritative parent after years of permissive parenting. However, Gabby's emerging challenges at age nine confirm the need for increased scaffolding to foster responsibility. Juanita refuses to handicap Gabby by oversheltering her further. Though the path ahead includes resistance and missteps, Juanita feels ready to parent Gabby with an authoritative blend of nurture and structure.

Chapter Two

Chapter 2: What's the Best Approach to Use for My Child?

In this chapter, we explore the essential aspects of guiding children's behavior with empathy and respect. Our strategy extends beyond simply instructing children on their actions. Instead, our goal is to cultivate within them a sense of worth and capability. This involves establishing clear, achievable expectations that align with their level of understanding and their developmental stage.

At the heart of our discussion is the creation of an environment where children feel acknowledged and comprehended. We stress the significance of transparent communication, where expectations are not only articulated but also explained and connected to the wider implications and relevance of their actions. This method assists children in grasping the rationale behind their behaviors, encouraging a more profound comprehension and assimilation of positive conduct.

We further examine the role of caregivers in consistently reinforcing these behaviors. Consistency here refers not merely to the frequency of rewards or consequences but also to being a steadfast source of guidance and support. It encompasses being available and responsive in a manner that bolsters the child's learning and development.

Additionally, this chapter investigates the importance of open and sincere dialogue. It's about forging a conversation with children in which their perspectives and emotions are acknowledged and their contributions are valued. Such communication is crucial in transforming behavioral guidance into a collaborative process, with children actively participating in their own growth.

Ultimately, this chapter presents a clear exploration of directing children toward positive behaviors through lucid, consistent, and communicative methods. It's about fostering growth not only through rules and structures but also through comprehension, empathy, and authentic interaction with the child's world.

Behavioral Expectations

Let's talk honestly about setting expectations for children. It's not about control or punishment. It's about guidance—showing them a path to being their best selves. We need to lay out goals clearly and make sure they're realistic. "Clean up your Legos when you're done playing"—that's doable. It builds accountability and pride. Speak respectfully and listen attentively—these expectations teach empathy. Small steps cultivate the confidence to take on bigger challenges. This is how children learn to trust themselves. By reinforcing these habits, they begin to understand the importance of responsibility and the satisfaction it brings. As they grow, they'll apply these principles in more complex situations, nurturing a sense of integrity and self-discipline.

For example, a child was leaving homework scattered all over instead of completing it. The parent and child agreed putting the work neatly away when done is reasonable. When they started following through, the parent highlighted how this responsibility helps the whole family. Meeting children where they are with practical expectations signals, "I believe in you." That validation itself motivates. It's not just about the homework; it's about nurturing a sense of belonging and contribution to the family. This approach shifts the focus from mere task completion to understanding the role of individual actions in the greater context of family life.

We have to meet them where they are developmentally. Setting the bar too high leads to frustration. Broken trust is hard to rebuild. Reasonable expectations tell our children, "I am on your team and want you to succeed." That validation stays with them. It's a message of love and respect, telling them they are capable and valued. This balance of challenge and support fosters resilience and self-esteem, equipping them to face future challenges with confidence.

Token Exchange System

The token system is concrete and fair. Each token marks an expectation met. The rewards are meaningful—extra playtime, a trip to the park, their favorite dinner. This teaches follow-through and consequence. More tokens equal a bigger reward, but everything is reasonable. It's not transactional. It shows that good choices add up to something worthwhile. Children learn to motivate themselves. They see their actions impact their world. This system isn't just about earning tokens; it's a lesson in cause and effect, showing that their actions have real, tangible outcomes. It reinforces the concept of delayed gratification, teaching them patience and long-term thinking.

For instance, a child struggled with consistently doing chores like feeding the pet. A reward chart was made where stickers were earned for remembering without reminders. Fun rewards like a movie night followed their sustained effort. This modeled how building good habits matters more than just the prize. The reward chart became a visual reminder of their progress and commitment, enhancing their sense of accomplishment. It's not just about the chores; it's about nurturing a sense of responsibility and care for others.

The excitement of "cashing in" tokens makes them feel capable. Giving children power over rewards builds autonomy. Over time, their motivation shifts from simple self-interest to real self-esteem. This empowerment is a cornerstone in developing self-driven, confident individuals. It's a journey from external motivation to discovering their internal drive. Ultimately, the goal is to foster a mindset where the joy of achieving is the reward in itself.

Consistency

Meet expectations with consistency, not rigidity. Respond predictably, whether good or bad. This provides security for children to grow. Show up emotionally, too, in joy and in frustration. Consistent caring teaches self-worth beyond achievements. It builds trust in unconditional support. Consistency is the bedrock for children to understand themselves and feel safe as they learn. This steady presence assures them that they are in a safe environment where they can experiment, make mistakes, and learn without fear of harsh judgment.

For example, with dinnertime tantrums over dessert, the parent responded calmly and firmly, reiterating the consistent rule. Despite repeated meltdowns, the child eventually accepted that "no means no" when enforcement is dependable. This teaches them the value of boundaries and the importance of respecting them. Through consistency, Children learn that rules aren't arbitrary but are there to guide and protect them.

When we're dependably present, children internalize that relationships can be reliable, too. This allows them to open up and be vulnerable without fear. Consistency over time beats insecurity and doubt. It's not just about enforcing rules; it's about being a reliable source of love and support. Children nurtured in such environments tend to develop strong emotional intelligence and secure attachments.

Communication

Talk with children, not at them. Explain why rules matter—how they affect others and themselves. Listen sincerely, too. Their input makes things stick. Encourage questions and concerns—this guides them much better than lectures. Share excitement about rewards. Let the children feel heard and involved. Communication makes the system real, not abstract. That connection motivates more than tokens. It's a two-way street, fostering a sense of partnership and mutual respect. This openness builds a foundation of trust, making children more receptive to guidance and advice.

For instance, a child kept forgetting sports gear, not due to irresponsibility but anxiety on game days. Simply asking "why" and listening openly led to uncovering and addressing the emotional root cause together. This approach shows children that their feelings and thoughts are valued, creating a safe space for honest conversations. It's about understanding, not just compliance.

Assumptions can be dangerous. Giving children a voice counters our biases about their motives. Listening builds empathy on both sides. Communication cements relationships in ways control never can. It's not just about solving the immediate problem; it's about nurturing a lifelong relationship based on mutual respect and understanding.

Gradual Fading

Independence needs gradual steps. As good habits settle in, external rewards can phase out. Space out tokens further apart. Replace them with praise—not false flattery, but real recognition of progress. Discuss feelings about ditching tokens. Guide children to feel fundamental satisfaction from good choices. This self-reinforcement sticks longer than any reward. Fading out tokens is about revealing the self-motivated child that's already there. This process respects their growing maturity and acknowledges their ability to make good choices without constant external incentives.

For example, a reward chart helped a child take ownership of their morning routine. After a time, they self-initiated stopping the formal rewards, feeling internally motivated by the positive momentum they created. This shift from external validation to internal satisfaction is a significant milestone in a child's development. It demonstrates their evolving understanding of self-discipline and personal responsibility.

It's not about quitting cold turkey. Make this transition collaborative—children will buy in to what they build. Independence can't be rushed, only nurtured over time with care. When children choose good for its own sake, they're on their way. This gradual approach ensures that the transition to self-motivation is smooth and natural, setting them up for lifelong success.

Apply It! Exercise: Building a Personalized Token System

Objective: This exercise is designed to help caregivers create a personalized token system that aligns with the principles of behavioral expectations, consistency, and effective communication.

Materials Needed:

- Paper and pens/pencils

- A variety of small tokens (e.g., stickers, stars, small cards)

- A list of potential rewards (can be activities, privileges, or tangible items)

Steps:

1. Identify and define behaviors: Sit down with the child and discuss the behaviors you would like to encourage. These should be specific, observable, and achievable actions, such as "sharing toys with siblings" or "completing homework on time." Write these behaviors down in simple language that the child can understand.

2. Explain the token system: Show the tokens to the child and explain how they can earn them by displaying the behaviors you've listed. Discuss with the child how many tokens each behavior is worth. This could vary depending on the difficulty or importance of the behavior.

3. Set up the reward system: Go through the list of potential rewards with the child. Decide together how many tokens each reward will cost. Make sure the rewards are desirable for

the child and that the "cost" is achievable. Write down this "token menu and keep it visible.

4. Role-playing: Engage in a role-playing activity where the child earns a token for a demonstrated behavior. This helps them understand the system in a practical, hands-on way. Also, role-play a scenario where they trade in tokens for a reward, emphasizing the joy and satisfaction of this exchange.

5. Discuss consistency and expectations: Talk about the importance of consistency in using the token system. Make it clear that tokens will be given reliably when the agreed-upon behaviors are observed. Also, discuss the gradual process of reducing reliance on tokens over time as positive behaviors become habitual.

6. Feedback and adjustment: At the end of the exercise, ask the child for their thoughts and feelings about the system. Be open to making adjustments based on their feedback, ensuring that the system feels fair and motivating to them.

7. Implementation: Start implementing the system, remembering to consistently award tokens and offer rewards as agreed. Regularly check in with the child to discuss the system and make any necessary adjustments.

8. Outcome: By the end of this exercise, the child should have a clear understanding of the token system, feel a sense of ownership and involvement in it, and be motivated to exhibit the positive behaviors outlined. The caregiver, in turn, will have established a practical tool for encouraging and reinforcing these behaviors in a consistent and communicative manner.

The Power of Praise and Encouragement in Shaping Behavior

As we guide and support our children through their developmental journey, the power of praise and encouragement stands out as an essential element. This holistic method, blending both words and actions, plays a crucial role in recognizing and positively reinforcing a child's behavior. More than mere acknowledgment, this approach is instrumental in boosting a child's self-esteem and drive.

Praise and encouragement are not merely about celebrating achievements; they are vital tools that empower the child. This empowerment lets children see the significance of their actions and their ripple effects. Such empowerment is crucial in guiding children toward taking responsibility for their actions and nurturing a strong sense of independence.

Furthermore, this approach transcends basic behavioral management. It lays the groundwork for a child's confidence and sense of worth. When children feel valued and acknowledged, they're more inclined to continue positive behaviors. This isn't driven by external incentives but by an internalization of these behaviors as part of their self-identity.

In essence, the utilization of praise and encouragement is a fundamental component in fostering positive behavior in children. It's a strategy that profoundly connects with them, motivating them to take charge of their actions and evolve into self-assured, responsible individuals. As caregivers, our adept use of these tools can profoundly impact a child's growth, influencing not just their actions but shaping their core identity.

Case Study: Shifting From Authoritarianism to Compassionate Guidance

Mia is a 36-year-old single mother to a 7-year-old son named Alex. As the only parent in a busy household, Mia struggled with anger and rigid authoritarian tactics trying to control Alex's strong-willed personality. After reading this chapter on empathetic, collaborative behavior guidance, Mia commits to evolving her approach.

Like the vignette of "John" in the Chapter 1 section on authoritarian parenting, Mia previously demanded obedience from Alex without open communication. For example, when he forgot homework assignments, she would yell, shame him as "irresponsible," and immediately institute harsh punishments like week-long groundings. Over time, this authoritarian approach produced anxiety and perfectionism in Alex despite good grades.

Alex grew withdrawn around Mia, only engaging when prompted, and never voluntarily expressing preferences or feelings. At parent/teacher conferences, Alex's second-grade teacher raised concerns about his lack of participation and low confidence. The teacher explained that authoritarian parenting often negatively impacts child development despite intentions to motivate.

Mia reflected deeply on her rigid tendencies, recognizing that while ensuring Alex's success academically, she had damaged his trust and self-esteem. She researched more positive behavior guidance strategies, getting input from counselors and other parents. Mia committed to abandoning her authoritarian approach for an authoritative nurturing and structure blend instead.

First, Mia instituted weekly family meetings to check in on major areas like school, activities, and home life. This regular open communication made Alex feel heard and respected. Second, Mia involved Alex in cocreating House Rules with related rewards and consequences. She focused on collaborative problem-solving when mistakes happened, not rushing to arbitrary punishments.

Finally, Mia consciously shifted her praise and corrections to reinforce positive values, not just critique negative behaviors. She emphasized effort over perfection, compassion over control, and integrity over mere obedience. Within months, Alex blossomed, regaining curiosity, self-confidence, and engagement under this supportive guidance system.

The changes didn't come easily with habits so engrained in Mia's instinctive reactions. But her commitment to Alex's healthy development fueled persistence. Gradually letting go of authoritarian control produced immense rewards. Alex began making responsible choices more independently, feeling intrinsically motivated and not compliant out of fear. He also started sharing spontaneously about his school life and interests.

This case illustrates how authoritative nurture balanced with structure can heal harm from pure authoritarian tactics. While Mia's original intent was academic success for Alex, her harsh approach impaired emotional security and trust essential for well-being. Her pivot toward collaborative communication and compassionate teaching cultivated cooperation and mutual understanding. Though requiring short-term discomfort confronting old habits, Mia's journey conveys hope for families to break destructive cycles. With a dedication to understanding their roots, while forging new patterns, caregivers can guide children's behavior in ways that empower growth.

Case Study: Evolving From Permissive to Authoritative Parenting

Gabriela is a 42-year-old single mother to 8-year-old Emma. Having left home at 16 due to a chaotic upbringing involving neglect, Gabriela strived to give Emma a childhood filled with abundant nurture and freedom. However, Emma has become entitled and defiant as she enters her middle school years.

Similar to the "Julie" example in the Chapter 1 section on permissive parents, Gabriela avoids upholding bedtimes, media rules, or homework structure to avoid conflict. She instantly yields to Emma's demands, whether regarding expensive impulse purchases or letting her skip school for trivial reasons. At recent parent/teacher meetings, Emma's teachers noted consistently incomplete work and distractedly clinging to peers.

Gabriela realized that her permissive, passive parenting produced in Emma a delay in maturity and a lack of work ethic or responsibility that is normally expected by this age. But afraid of damaging their close bond through discipline, Gabriela continued resorting to bribes to get Emma to cooperate. This approach resulted in worsening entitled attitudes and disrespect.

However, a breaking point hit when Emma began dangerous preteen risky behaviors like sneaking out late and shoplifting with peers. Gabriela recognized that without firmer scaffolding, Emma seemed at risk for substance abuse or pregnancy, given her poor decisions amid pressure to fit in. Gabriela committed to gaining skills for authoritative guidance, not sparing Emma from consequences in the name of friendship.

First, Gabriela created House Rules addressing everything from homework needs to media usage to contributions around the home.

She presented these to Emma, allowing some collaborative input to build investment but refusing to relinquish nonnegotiables regarding safety and ethics. They jointly made a "responsibilities chart" that would yield rewards when upheld.

Second, Gabriela prepared to respond decisively to testing limits about following rules through these transitions. She let Emma feel the sting of reasonable, proportional results from broken commitments without rescuing her. Gabriela also required counseling so Emma could build skills, escape negative peer influence, and establish better decision-making skills during early adolescence.

Finally, Gabriela scheduled daily check-ins to reinforce open communication channels rather than demands and disengagement. She proactively reviewed social events and agreements about alcohol, curfews, and other dynamics requiring vigilance. Gabriela felt equipped with bottom lines that could save Emma from trauma while conveying unconditional love beneath a firmer structure.

This case study illustrates the common struggle to shift away from solely a friend role into a parenting mentor for a child's benefit. Gabriela's choice to establish consistency, boundaries, and collaborative support launched Emma's maturity. It also transformed their relationship, cementing trust through Gabriela's refusal to abdicate protective guidance when tempted to prolong childhood with overpermissiveness. Her journey conveys that through authoritative nurturing and limits, caregivers can shepherd their children responsibly into adolescence.

Chapter Three

Chapter 3: A Healthy Expression of Emotions

When we look deeply into our children's hearts, we discover entire worlds alive with emotion. As parents, nurturing those complex inner landscapes is our sacred duty.

Through years of working with families, I've seen that a child's emotional health stems largely from the environments and communication patterns we expose them to daily. This isn't about perfectly scripted conversations but, instead, about listening with raw presence.

In the following pages, I share hard-won wisdom on fostering emotional intelligence in children—ideas like teaching nuanced feeling words, validating emotions, and creating inclusive routines where all parts belong. Still, concepts mean little without inner shift.

My intention isn't just to offer more tools to cram onto your full plates. It's inviting relief by changing how we view emotions overall—as insight rather than interference, as connectivity rather than correction. When we can embrace the full spectrum of a feeling without resistance, we can embrace our children more completely, too.

If emotions emanate from the heart, then may we parent from the heart as well—with abundant love, patience, forgiveness, and humanity. Will you join me in this humble and sacred space?

Open Communication

Encourage open and honest communication. Create a safe and non-judgmental environment where children feel comfortable expressing their feelings. Let them know that all emotions are okay, even the messy ones we want to avoid. Validate their feelings even if you disagree with the behavior. We have to meet them where they are. Practice active listening with your full presence when children want to share. To ensure connection, pay attention, ask clarifying questions if needed, and reflect back what you heard. Avoid dismissing or judging their emotions, as the only purpose this will serve is to have them disconnect from you and shut down. This is vulnerable work for both parent and child.

Bring up emotions naturally in everyday conversations. Ask how situations or events made them feel—the good and the bad. Share your own emotional reactions sometimes, too. We are all in this together. Look for changes in behavior that could signal hidden feelings. Gently create opportunities to talk without pressure. Meet them where they are. If they aren't ready, they aren't ready. That's okay, too. This is about support, not force.

Start with the small daily feelings. A toy breaking may not seem like a big deal, but it's practice for the bigger stuff later about identity and relationships. Listen well today, so they will talk to you tomorrow. Remain patient because you cannot force timelines around vulnerability. Let conversations happen in their own time. Keep creating a safe space rather than demanding deep sharing. Protect that space with nonjudgment. Growth will happen organically if we nurture the seeds properly.

The key is consistency in meeting them where they are developmentally and gently encouraging more openness over time through compassion and listening. Perfection is not required for this sacred work.

Teach Emotional Vocabulary

Help children identify and label their swirling emotions. Teach them a nuanced feeling vocabulary so they can better express the complexity inside. We have to name it before we can tame it, as they say. Start with their surface emotions and guide them to go deeper. Why does this situation trigger that anger, hurt, or shame? The whys matter immensely. Keep asking gentle questions to understand the roots. It builds self-awareness and connection. This is a gift.

Use feeling words often in your home. Name your own emotions, too. Say, "I feel frustrated," rather than just yelling. Model how to articulate big feelings for little hearts. Write down new feeling words they overhear and discuss them together. What does exasperated mean? How is that different from angry? Normalize the entire human spectrum. All emotions are allowed, even the uncomfortable ones we want to avoid.

When a child shuts down in stubbornness, approach with compassion about the underlying emotions. Say, "It seems like you have some big feelings happening. I get like that too sometimes." Teach that all feelings are allowed, but certain actions are not. Separate the emotion from behavior. Make space to process the emotion first with patient listening. Then, revisit the behavior once felt.

This is a pillar you'll return to often as part of raising emotionally intelligent children. It starts early and weaves through conversations as they grow. Over time, a rich emotional vocabulary becomes second nature. It allows them to develop self-awareness, express needs, and communicate clearly within relationships. The words we impart become the tools they'll use to courageously craft a meaningful life. This work matters in our noisy world.

Lead by Example

Demonstrate healthy emotional expression in your own behavior. Children often learn by observing us. They study our reactions closely, mirroring what they see. We must model the same openness we want to impart. Name your feelings, sit with discomfort, and confess mistakes. Show up authentically and let them witness the journey firsthand. The emotional pathways we pave become their footsteps in time.

When you catch yourself hiding pain or glossing over anger, circle back to process it together. Explain what you learned for next time. Growth means progress, not perfection. We cannot expect brave vulnerability from our children if we don't stand courageously on our own. This is sacred work that requires self-honesty, humility, and forgiveness.

Provide Artistic Outlets

Offer creative ways for children to express roiling emotions, like drawing, painting, or writing. Art can be a powerful tool for release when words fail us. Encourage free artistic expression without judgment on outcomes. Provide a listening space for them to share about their art only if they choose. Creativity both unlocks inner wisdom and builds self-confidence.

Display their art prominently in your home if they permit—not to flaunt talent but to honor expression. Surround them with visible reminders that all emotions deserve space. Frame their emotional bravery for all to appreciate. Each artistic risk empowers their developing voices.

Encourage Journaling

For older children, keeping a journal allows them to process emotions through writing. Externalizing inner thoughts by putting pencil to paper brings clarity. Journals are also time capsules, locking in memories and charting personal growth. Treat a child's journal as a sacred text by respecting privacy unless pages are specifically shared.

When journaling together, pose occasional open-ended prompts about meaningful events, struggles, joys, and dreams. Not to pry but to normalize self-reflection. Writing often unearths new layers of self-awareness that conversations miss. If journaling independently, convey your availability to discuss anything they write if they ever wish. Hold this space without expectation.

Physical Activity

Engage in physical activities together as a family. Exercise releases pent-up energy and stress, promoting emotional balance. Shoot hoops in the driveway, dance in the living room, and go for bike rides. Connect joyfully while also moving your bodies. Laughter doubles as cardio when spirits run high. End each activity with a grounded conversation about the emotions felt before, during, and after. Did frustration shift to pride? Anxiety to calm? This builds awareness.

Also, discuss how physical health and emotional health are interconnected and how food fuels us not just physically but mentally. How sleep and exercise impact mood and mindset. Demonstrate this holistic connection through your lifestyle and conversations. Help them listen to the wisdom of their bodies. Intuitive signals come when we tune out distraction and tune into sensation.

Mindfulness and Relaxation

Teach children simple mindfulness or relaxation techniques for emotional regulation, like deep belly breathing, visualization, or quiet meditation. Start young when attention spans are short. Just one minute of mindful breathing can recalibrate the nervous system when emotions intensify. Make it playful at first, leading guided imagery journeys or going on mindfulness scavenger hunts outside. Over time, these tools will inoculate them against life's turmoil.

In our fast-paced society, stillness is a radical act, yet it grounds and centers us inwardly, even if just for a few moments. Give your full presence when practicing mindfulness together. Your commitment demonstrates its power more than words alone. With increasing anxiety and depression across younger generations, these centering traditions offer refuge. It all begins by simply slowing down and tuning in.

Validate Their Feelings

Acknowledge and validate your child's emotions without trying to change or fix them. Say, "I hear how sad that makes you feel. I would feel sad, too, if that happened." Let them know that the full range of human emotion is allowed, seen, and held with compassion here. There are no bad feelings—all are welcome. This emotional validation builds trust and resilience. It shows them that negative spaces will not be avoided.

Children are like emotional detectives, navigating inner landscapes with curiosity and wonder when conditions are safe enough. Provide validation frequently in small moments so it becomes second nature when big emotions swell later about identity, relationships, purpose, and loss. The ultimate goal is for them to internalize self-validation as they grow. But first, they must observe and experience this as it is modeled by you with compassion.

Set Realistic Expectations

Help children understand that experiencing the full range of emotions is part of being human. Expect ups and downs, good days as well as bad. You must be willing to hold yourself to this perspective. When we expect constant joy or ease, normal negative emotions signal failure instead of dimensional living. Provide guidance, empathy, and tools for navigating both peaks and valleys with increasing agility over time. There are no shortcuts to resilience or skipping straight to gratitude. But we walk together when the terrain gets rocky.

Also, avoid sheltering children from all of life's messiness. Over-protection breeds fragility, not strength. Let them skin some knees, get their hearts broken, fail, and try again. You can still offer bandages or a listening ear. The lessons sink deeper when learned firsthand. Guide but don't hide reality. Your role is to build resilient copers, not create fragile bubbles.

Problem-Solving Skills

Teach simple problem-solving tactics to address sources of stress at appropriate ages. Name the problem, brainstorm solutions, evaluate options, and test choices. Of course tackle the process for them when young, then transfer ownership as skills develop. Even small dilemmas like fighting with friends or getting stuck on homework contain seed lessons about confronting difficulty. Guide but don't rescue. Struggle today strengthens muscles for greater challenges tomorrow.

Remember, problem-solving itself is a skill requiring repetition to engrain neural pathways. Break tasks down into steps. Start simple. Just like any coaching opportunity, expect messiness as competence builds. Praise effort over outcomes, which focuses them inward. Avoid shaming when they struggle, which focuses them outward. Meet them where they are developmentally and scaffold the next reachable stretch.

Establish Routines

Consistent family routines provide a sense of loving stability amidst outer chaos. children thrive when they know what to expect—both the warm joy of connection and the gentle security of structure. Of course, allow flexibility, too! Rigidity fractures under pressure. Infuse grace into your routines and modify accordingly with age or changing needs. Hold space at the dinner table, read books before bedtime, and share gratitude at sunrise. Rituals rooted in meaning outlast rules rooted in control.

When children help cocreate family routines, ownership increases engagement. Have a meeting to decide on meaningful rituals together. Which current routines nourish their spirits? What new habits might foster connection? Welcome their input and ideas. Compromise if certain suggestions stretch too far for you right now. Revisit and refine routines together as all needs shift. What was once cement can become clay again. Through it all, anchor back to shared purpose and love.

Social Support

Foster healthy relationships between your child and their friends, classmates, teachers, relatives, mentors, and faith communities. Having an extensive support system provides mirrors reflecting back their goodness when they cannot see it themselves. It also gives companions to laugh, cry, and grow alongside. They also provide alternative perspectives different from your own. Advocate for your child to both receive and give love within their widening social circles.

Also, reach out when you see your child struggling socially or emotionally. Consult school counselors, therapists, pediatricians, coaches, or trusted clergy. It takes a village to raise a child, as the African proverb goes. Do not isolate or attempt to handle mental health challenges alone. There are so many compassionate professionals who want to help and who offer tools we may lack. Seek support early when worries emerge. Strong foundations prevent bigger cracks later.

Model Healthy Coping

Demonstrate self-compassion when you get frustrated. Say out loud, "This is really hard right now. What do I need? I'm going to take some deep breaths first." Show children how taking breaks, resting the body, writing in a journal, talking to a friend, or seeing a counselor can help process difficult emotions. Name the coping strategies that work for you. They will emulate and explore their own in time. But first, they require demonstrations.

Make space for the full rainbow of human emotions. When you suppress certain feelings like anger, sadness, or disappointment, children learn that those parts of themselves must also remain hidden. Give overt permission for the darkness along with light. Shadows are lost when banished, not integrated. Wholeness requires excavating buried aspects of self, too. Demonstrate this emotional archaeology.

Encourage Empathy

Expand children's emotional intelligence by discussing how others experience the world and how it feels to walk in another's shoes. Read diverse books, have courageous dinner conversations, and volunteer together to serve those facing hardship. When conflicts inevitably arise with friends or classmates, guide children to reflect on multiple perspectives before reacting. What is that person feeling and why? What could help the relationship become whole? Empathy maps a path beyond bitterness when nourished young.

Emphasize justice over judgment. Judgment separates and punishes. "You did something wrong, so you're grounded." Justice seeks to understand the roots of behavior and restore harmony. "Your actions hurt your sister. What happened today, and how can we work to heal things?" Justice is a process, not a verdict. Model this distinction through your disciplinary approach.

Remember, each child has a unique emotional topography. Sensitive children will require additional nurturing of their inner landscape to prevent overwhelm. High-energy children need more outlets for fire containment. Observe closely and meet them where they are, but keep leading everyone a bit further over time. Growth happens at the edge of comfort. Create an atmosphere of radical listening and acceptance so emotions become allies, not adversaries, within your precious family.

Apply It! Mapping Your Child's Emotional Landscape

A useful way to understand and connect with your child's inner emotional world is to create a visual map of their feelings. Here's a simple yet illuminating activity:

Materials Needed:

- Blank paper or poster board

- Markers, colored pencils, or crayons

- Arts & craft supplies (optional)

Instructions:

1. Find some quiet time to reflect on your child. Consider their emotional patterns. What feelings do they express most frequently? What situations or events trigger difficult emotions for them? When do they seem most joyful and engaged?

2. On your blank page, draw a large outline of a landscape shape with valleys, mountains, rivers, etc. This will become a symbolic map of your child's emotional world.

3. Label different parts of the landscape map with specific emotions your child experiences. You can name both positive and negative feelings. Use your knowledge of their triggers and reactions.

4. Color code each emotion area on the map. For example, shade anger in red and joyful emotions in yellow. Get creative with craft materials to embellish.

5. Add symbols or draw scenes around the map that represent situations tied to various feelings. Maybe a playground for happiness or dark clouds hovering over anger.

6. Once it is complete, share this landscape map with your child. Ask them to modify it to reflect their inner emotional experience accurately. Make it cocreated.

7. Post your emotional landscape map in a visible spot. Revisit it together when conflicts arise to increase connection and understanding. Update the map as your child's emotional world evolves.

This hands-on awareness exercise models that all emotions are valid and valued here. It opens conversations around healthy feelings, expression, and self-understanding. Use this activity as one of many bridges into your child's developing inner world.

Listening and Connecting with Your Child's Developing Emotional World

What children most require is our authentic presence—seeing, listening, and accepting them fully, even when their storms rage outside our paradigms. By bearing witness without judgment, their storms subside organically. Space held gently allows feelings to transform into insight.

Of course, we will still falter amidst the beauty and messiness. I certainly do! But we can do it with more empathy, more courage, and more slowing down for connection over correction. We are all still learning how to be fully human and how to feel deeply without getting lost in emotion. We are all finding our way together each new day.

May you feel equipped yet gently unburdened as your family moves ahead on this winding path. When doubt or fatigue sets in, as it surely will, pause and recall your child's luminous eyes—how they shine with implicit trust in your guidance. This love is always stronger than struggle. You've been a caring guide all along.

Case Study: From Emotional Neglect to Connection

Ava is a 7-year-old only child being raised by a single father, Marco. Since Ava's mom left when she was a baby, Marco struggled profoundly as the sole caregiver while grieving this loss. Emotionally drained and lacking support, he detached from Ava over the years.

Marco met Ava's basic needs but worked long hours and stayed distracted during their little shared downtime. He avoided emotional conversations, dismissing her worries as unimportant or dramatic. When Ava got upset, Marco reacted impatiently rather than listening, saying she was "too sensitive." Ava learned to cry alone and mask feelings around her father.

A preschool teacher first raised concerns about Ava's flat emotional affect, lack of engagement with peers, and poor language development. Marco felt surprised and ashamed to realize that Ava likely modeled his emotional unavailability. Her teacher explained that without intervention, these early childhood attachment gaps could impact Ava's mental health and relationships long-term.

Marco began reading books about childhood emotional neglect and ways to rebuild connection through attunement. He committed to showing up differently despite exhaustion and past trauma. Marco utilized tips from this chapter, like making space for Ava to express all feelings without judgment. He worked on validating her emotions by saying things like, "I hear how sad you feel. I would feel sad, too, if that happened."

Additionally, Marco took Ava to play therapy, which presented revelations about her sense of loneliness. This counseling equipped Marco with tailored strategies to nurture Ava's unfolding inner world. He instituted regular one-on-one time, including feeling check-ins and creative outlets like art and journaling to strengthen their bond. During this dedicated space for emotional connection, he witnessed Ava brighten through consistent compassion.

As their relationship deepened, Marco also opened up appropriately to Ava about his own grief and depressive periods after losing her mom. He became vulnerable about past struggles, showing up emotionally. Marco described his commitment to breaking generational cycles so she feels safe to express all parts of herself.

Over time, her preschool teacher observed huge positive shifts in Ava's demeanor, confidence, and peer interactions. Ava began proudly sharing her artwork depicting various emotions. She learned to articulate upset feelings directly to Marco rather than shut down. Their newfound emotional attunement equipped Ava to communicate her needs and nurtured secure attachment.

While their relationship remains a continuing work in progress requiring mutual effort, the shifts Marco implemented by embracing nurturance versus detachment made a profound difference in helping Ava heal and thrive. Their story conveys hope for any parent to form a securely attached relationship when gaps exist early on. With dedication to emotional attunement and unconditional presence, caregivers hold the power to fundamentally shape a child's development.

Case Study: Cultivating Resilience

Miguel is the passionate, creative 8-year-old son of Marissa, a loving yet anxiety-prone single mom. Miguel and Marissa endured significant hardship when Miguel's father abandoned them two years ago, leaving Marissa to work long hours alone, supporting her son.

As the only parent, Marissa struggled to convey emotional stability while quietly facing her own depression. When Miguel expressed sadness about his dad's absence, Marissa tended to react with fear that "something was wrong" rather than calmly listening. She constantly worried Miguel couldn't handle setbacks.

A school counselor advised Marissa that avoiding discussions about loss denied Miguel opportunities to process grief and gain coping skills. children model resilience when guided in expressing difficult emotions. By rupturing each time Miguel got upset, his emotional muscles stayed weak.

Marissa recognized that her panic about "protecting" Miguel from negative feelings actually handicapped his resilience. She consulted this book's tips about validating all emotions without trying to fix pain. Marissa committed to staying present through Miguel's discomfort, demonstrating confidence that he could integrate these experiences rather than fall apart.

She also role-modeled healthy regulation of her own big feelings. Marissa openly discussed coping strategies that worked for her, like journaling, exercising, seeing a counselor, and relying on the community. Bit by bit, Miguel mirrored these wellness practices, discovering self-care outlets that resonated with his creative spirit.

Over months of Marissa moving through anxiety to offer calm attunement first, Miguel gained trust, sharing vulnerable parts of himself. He began expressing sadness, confusion, and even anger about his dad's abandonment. Marissa absorbed these complex emotions without fear or judgment.

In time, Miguel started volunteering his writings, songs, and art around loss and resilience. Marissa responded with love and praise for his developing wisdom. She frequently reminded Miguel of his inherent strength and worth regardless of his father's limitations. His emotional muscles grew.

This case powerfully demonstrates how children model resilience when caregivers guide them through the full range of human emotion rather than avoid pain for overprotection. By progressing from panic to presence, Marissa equipped Miguel to transmute darkness into light through creative expressions. He now moves through life with increasing confidence, empathy, and leadership, enriched by having journeyed courageously "into the depths" even at a young age alongside his mother's steady compassion.

Chapter Four

Chapter 4: Praise and Encouragement

As parents, our words hold immense power—both to nurture our children's self-confidence and extinguish their inner light if used carelessly. That's why purposeful, positive praise serves as a pivotal tool for supporting developmental growth. When children hear their efforts, achievements, and character explicitly affirmed, it builds an unshakable foundation of self-belief.

In this chapter, we will explore specific, descriptive praise focusing on concrete actions over vague platitudes. You'll learn the importance of sincerity, encouragement that emphasizes progress, and communicating praise through verbal and nonverbal alignment. We'll also get creative brainstorming varied approaches beyond the cliché "Good job!" to inspire children through our words.

While praising effectively takes intention and skill, its motivational impact makes the effort more than worthwhile. Our words can spur children to tackle new challenges, persevere despite obstacles, and develop lasting self-esteem stemming from internal wells of knowledge about their inherent value. Let's get started filling up those wells!

The Power of Specific Praise

Offering praise is one of the most powerful tools we have as parents to encourage desired behaviors and nurture our children's self-confidence. But generic praises like "well done!" often ring hollow. Children see right through vague platitudes when their specific actions aren't recognized.

That's why specific praise focused on concrete behaviors makes a bigger motivational impact. Rather than just saying, "You did a nice drawing," try, "I see you combined many different colors to create texture—great blending work!" When noticing helpful behaviors, spell out exactly what actions you want to reinforce.

- Here are some examples:

- "Thank you for clearing all your toys off the family room floor when I asked. That was very responsible."

- "I saw you sat patiently through your brother's entire guitar practice session. I know that takes focus and self-control."

- "You wrote this entire story all on your own with a clear beginning, middle, and end. Great organizational skills!"

The beauty of specific praise is it builds self-awareness in children about what they did well while making abstract concepts like responsibility and patience concrete. So catch those little moments of progress and describe back explicitly what type of praises you see.

Watch your child's motivation and confidence flourish when their good efforts shine clearly under the spotlight of your words.

The Motivational Power of Timely Rewards

In addition to specific praise, recognizing positive behaviors quickly is key for reinforcement. When you notice a child doing something you want to encourage, offer acknowledgment immediately rather than waiting. This builds the neural connections between actions and results.

For example, saying, "Connor, wonderful job sitting quietly while Mommy was on the phone!" right after the good behavior occurs is aptly timed. Waiting to praise until hours or days later loses some motivational traction. They need to see progress recognized in real time.

An effective strategy many families use is a "Responsibility Chart" to track behaviors throughout the week. This can take the form of a simple poster board with columns for each day and rows assigned to different positive habits like getting ready promptly, completing chores, etc. Let children decorate their own charts!

Each time they demonstrate the desired behavior that day, they earn a star, sticker, or checkmark in that box. At the end of the week, accumulated rewards are exchanged for meaningful privileges or experiences, not money. This teaches intrinsic value. Possible rewards include special one-on-one time with parents, a movie night where they pick the show, extra tablet time, choosing weekend activities, etc.

By monitoring progress across time and exchanging points for things children genuinely want, you reinforce positive habits through healthy incentives children can see unfolding daily. It also provides joyful opportunities to—you guessed it—offer specific praise!

The Authenticity of Genuine Praise

Children have highly attuned radars for sincerity. They can sense when verbal affirmation comes from the heart rather than just being transactional. This instinctive authenticity meter starts developing early.

Consider how a toddler beams when you exclaim, "You did it!" after their first shaky steps. They intrinsically feel your delight. Now imagine casually muttering, "Good job, kiddo..." while distracted by your phone. The emotional impact nosedives.

As children grow, that radar only becomes more refined. They know when praise reflects true admiration rather than empty accolades to achieve compliance.

So, be mindful of both the quality and integrity of the praise you offer. Make eye contact and voice warm enthusiasm to affirm achievements like learning a new skill or overcoming a challenge. In moments of misbehavior, calmly redirect rather than offering hollow praise just to keep the peace.

When parents take time to notice and validate children's efforts with sincerity, it makes a world of difference in bolstering self confidence from the inside out. The key is ensuring that your words align with authentic emotional experience, not just saying the "right thing." Back up verbal praise by being fully present. The feelings will naturally follow.

Praising Effort and Perseverance

Rather than just celebrating end results, shift emphasis onto effort, improvement, and perseverance along the way. Remind children that major goals are achieved through many incremental steps, not overnight success. Praise their stamina when facing challenges.

For example, if cleaning their room feels daunting, don't wait until every last item gets put away perfectly to offer applause. Recognize mini-milestones instead—praise getting started on clothes, then acknowledge moving on to papers. Say something like, "I know you were feeling overwhelmed, but you took the first step of making your bed neatly. Now the room looks more organized already. Way to push past frustration!"

Sit with them during big tasks and guide them to break them down into more manageable pieces. Offer encouragement after each component step. "You finished sorting your toys first. Great system with bins! Now, let's clear papers off the floor together before tackling clothes. Smaller steps get us there."

Remind them that nobody succeeds alone. Everyone needs assistance, especially when learning new skills. Collaborate on strategies, then shine the spotlight on diligence and teamwork. Celebrate both solo miles and assisted progress. This conveys that the journey of growth is long, requiring community support. Their effort deserves appreciation at every step, not just at the summit.

Conveying Praise Through Body Language

When verbally praising children, your nonverbal signals should align positively, too. Back up spoken affirmations with body language that radiates warmth and approval.

For example, smile widely when commenting on how they persevered in solving a difficult puzzle. Let your facial expression communicate admiration. Offer a high five or thumbs up when they follow instructions promptly to convey "Great job!" visually, too.

Use enthusiastic tones paired with affirmative head nods or pats on the back to physically validate achievements like learning new academic skills or demonstrating responsibility. Make eye contact and lean in to display an engaged presence.

But beware of praise-diminishing mannerisms like distracted gazes at phones, indifferent shrugs, or cringing frowns when they proudly announce accomplishments. Even loving words lose luster if bodies communicate apathy, irritation, or dismissal. The two need alignment.

Think of yourself as a human amplification system for every bright moment you genuinely want to spotlight. Let positivity beam through your voice, gaze, and touch. Children always benefit from feeling psychologically seen and celebrated across channels of communication. Surround them with encouragement made visible and tangible through unified verbiage and body language. Let it sink in holistically.

Getting Creative

With

Praise

While descriptive praise focused on concrete actions is highly effective, children also thrive on receiving positive affirmations about their character and potential, too. Vary your praise approaches by incorporating

- Descriptive praise: Compliment specific behaviors as they happen. Describe what they did well, from cleaning up messes to speaking respectfully to producing good quality work in school. Make the actions you want repeated visible through words.

- Affirming language: Offer encouraging words about their talents and positively frame setbacks as learning opportunities. Remind them of their superpowers—things they bring to this world. Let them know you believe in their potential.

- Process praise: Highlight effort and perseverance unfolding day by day. "I'm proud of the way you stayed focused this week memorizing vocabulary." Don't just wait until end goals get achieved to offer praise.

Adapt methods to suit changing needs, but make praise a steady stream, not an occasional rain shower. All forms water seeds of confidence and self-esteem over time. Descriptive, affirming, and process-focused praise all help children internalize self-motivation rather than depending wholly on external validation.

So, diversify your praise portfolio! Combine tailored, unique language about strengths with frequent encouragement emphasizing progress over perfection. Watch all types lift your child up.

Apply It! Creative Ways to Praise

Praising children effectively takes some thought and creativity. Let's brainstorm fresh ways you can recognize your child's efforts and achievements.

Grab some art supplies, markers, and magazines, and make a praise collage! Follow these steps:

1. Cut out words and phrases from magazines related to topics like perseverance, accomplishments, character strengths, etc.

2. On a blank page, write headings like "Descriptive Praise," "Affirming Words," "Celebrating Progress," and "Encouragement."

3. Start a visual collage by pasting inspiring words and images under the various praise categories. Get creative with drawings, stickers, and color coding, too.

4. Add spaces to later fill in specific examples tailored to your child, like praising kindness, effort on a science fair project, learning to ride a bike, etc.

5. Hang this growing praise collage somewhere visible as inspiration for varied encouragement. Revisit it when you need fresh ideas or are struggling to praise effectively. Add new examples over time.

Turning praise into a hands-on piece of artwork makes the act of affirming children more concrete while building a supportive creativity habit together. When done collaboratively, designing this collage actually models descriptive, process, and strengths-based praise in real time too!

So gather supplies and put those creative thinking caps on. Let's start appreciating the blessing these children are in imaginative new ways!

Positive Affirmation Through Praise

As we close this chapter, I hope you feel confident in your praising abilities moving forward. While an infinite number of affirming statements exist, just remember the foundational principles of specificity, sincerity, and encouraging effort. Apply these guidelines fluidly based on your child's ever-evolving needs.

Most importantly, don't worry about praising "perfectly"—instead, praise authentically. Let encouragement flow naturally from a heart filled with care rather than angst over formal techniques. Perfectionism paralyzes progress, but compassion sets it free.

Our children require praise not because they are fragile but because all humans thrive when their gifts are spotted and validated. So take note of special strengths with mindfulness, then put admiration into words. If emotions ever constrain expression, let hugs speak for you. Truly loving children well through encouragement is not about what we say but how present we are in each moment—seeing their light clearly no matter what.

Case Study: Building Confidence Through Praise

Eva is a shy 8-year-old who struggles with low self-esteem. Though quite talented at drawing and painting, she rarely believes her artwork measures up. She also feels intimidated trying new physical activities like dance or soccer, scared of looking clumsy and embarrassing herself. Eva wants to participate but often retreats to isolated activities instead due to a lack of confidence.

Her mother, Amy, recognized that Eva would benefit from increased focused praise and encouragement to help build self-assurance. Rather than offering vague affirmations like "Good job!" Amy applied principles from this chapter to offer descriptive, specific praise regarding Eva's strengths.

During art projects, Amy took note of the unique color combinations Eva chose, saying things like, "I love how you blended the green and yellow to make this magical forest!" She also spotlighted Eva's perseverance, praising small milestones on bigger creations. Amy said, "You got the sky's base color down beautifully. Now let's think about some wispy white clouds to add dimension."

Regarding sports, Amy knew she needed to encourage brave first steps, trying new physical hobbies rather than waiting for mastery to offer praise. She focused applause on participation and effort over skill level. Phrases like "I'm proud of you for showing up even when it felt scary!" reinforced that courage and engagement mattered more than performance outcomes when building confidence.

Additionally, Amy utilized the Responsibility Chart method from this chapter. She created a poster board with a column assigned to each day of the week. Eva decorated it with colorful stickers and glitter. Together, they wrote desired behaviors to track, like helping with dishes, tidying her room, and feeding her pets. Eva earned a star sticker on her chart each time she demonstrated these actions without reminders. By Friday, she got to pick fun mother/daughter activities as rewards.

This visible system allowed Amy to offer frequent specific praise every time she caught Eva completing expected tasks. Citing exact behaviors like "Thank you for clearing the table without me asking!" reinforced the power of responsibility while highlighting effort through descriptive encouragement.

Over several months, Eva made huge strides in self-confidence thanks to her mother's purposeful praise. Her certainty as an artist blossomed beautifully. She also took risks pursuing new hobbies, staying motivated by intrinsic joy over talent judgments. Eva came to understand through Amy's affirmations that progress via perseverance matters more than instant success when building skills.

This case study demonstrates that with loving support helping spotlight children's strengths and consistent verbal encouragement emphasizing small wins, even shy children can gain the self-assurance needed to unlock their potential. While not overnight transformation, Eva's story conveys that over time, descriptive and sincere praise builds an unshakable foundation, equipping children to share their gifts confidently with the world.

Case Study: Building Jackson's Motivation Through Encouragement

Jackson is a bright yet distractible 10-year-old who rushes through school assignments, earning only average grades despite understanding concepts quickly when focused. His lack of effort especially shows in subjects less interesting to him, like writing. Jackson knows the material but believes he just "isn't good" at these topics, so he disengages.

His father, Tyler, recognized that Jackson needed consistent encouragement emphasizing diligence over innate talent to motivate him to try his best. Rather than generic platitudes, occasionally saying. "Nice job," Tyler committed to descriptive process praise per this chapter's tips. He decided to highlight Jackson's positive incremental progress to reinforce that persistence pays off academically too.

When tackling a challenging homework assignment, Tyler made an effort to track mini accomplishments, praising each component step completed. During a history paper, he said things like, "Your topic sentence clearly sets up the essay goal—nice job laying that foundation!" and "I see you added several supporting details next—that depth strengthens your case."

Rather than waiting until Jackson fully finished drafts, Tyler spotlighted his steady efforts throughout. He reminded Jackson that everyone requires help sharpening skills, especially on difficult tasks. Tyler suggested asking the teacher for proofreading advice later to model seeking constructive feedback.

At report card time, when Jackson's average writing grade first showed modest improvement, Tyler praised not the average score itself but the fact that Jackson persevered through multiple drafts until satisfied. Tyler said, "I'm proud of you for sticking with it, following through on revisions, and not giving up when it got tough."

To help efficiency in mastering boring topics, Tyler collaborated with Jackson to break assignments into mini-goals, jointly developing checklist schedules. Tyler reinforced focusing on each smaller step patiently rather than rushing. He promised to acknowledge every box completed. Tic marks visibly tracked progress.

While Jackson's work ethic remains a continued effort in progress, Tyler's specificity in spotlighting little wins has increased his motivation and self-confidence gradually. Jackson recognizes that his dad's encouraging process focus conveys belief in his inner persistence. He understands that steady effort earns genuine praise more than inborn talent. This fuels his self-efficacy to pursue interests passionately through inevitable obstacles. Tyler's descriptive encouragement has nurtured Jackson's growth mindset beautifully.

This case exemplifies how children bloom motivationally when parents shine attention on concrete efforts more than outcomes. Descriptive process praise grounds intrinsic value, reminding children that they have agency over results with perseverant grit. Rather than offering random "good jobs," specific encouragement aligned to children's developmental reality inspires best.

Chapter Five

Chapter 5: Teaching Social Intelligence

Even from toddlerhood, young children often gravitate toward asserting their own desires first, with limited ability to consider others' needs and experiences. Yet nurturing core values of sharing, empathy, and cooperation lays critical emotional foundations that blossom into generous spirits benefiting society long-term.

In the following pages, we will explore everyday opportunities for modeling inclusive behaviors ourselves while guiding children toward embracing these prosocial habits. You'll discover sample narratives for praising generosity when displayed organically, tips for structured activities that require taking turns, reflecting on impact, and collaborating toward common goals. We'll also discuss using stories, role-playing, and experiential learning to exercise empathetic muscles.

While these concepts remain complex for young developing minds, patiently planting seeds through demonstration, celebration, and consistency will allow compassion to slowly take root. Through reciprocal love and care, our children come to intuitively extend what they receive. Let us foster this first within families, then watch it spill into communities far beyond home.

Fostering the Art of Sharing

Sharing does not come naturally to young children who view possessions as extensions of self. Yet grasping this social skill lays the foundations for generosity, compromise, and community building. Lead by modeling inclusive behaviors. Demonstrate sharing in daily life. Take turns choosing games and take turns fairly while playing. Offer part of your snack saying "Here's some for you!" Use mealtimes to distribute food amongst family, saying things like, "Let's all finish one before having another." Narrate sharing actions openly. Make space for each person's needs to be considered.

Spot spontaneous sharing and praise it. When children display compromise by offering a coveted toy midplay, encourage that impulse. "Lily, Farah looks so happy that you shared your doll with her!" Then reciprocate sharing back to reinforce. Share something of yours back as an appreciation for their generosity.

Use stories and role play to illustrate sharing benefits. For example, read picture books showcasing cooperation, then dramatize scenarios about asking to borrow items or losing a toy, exploring resolution together. Tie it all back to how sharing creates a possibility for both short-term joy and deeper long-term relationships. Highlight the value for all. Discuss how sharing made the characters feel happier and more connected.

While young children remain self-focused, modeling inclusive behaviors combined with positive reinforcement for displays of generosity teaches that sharing can feel intrinsically rewarding. Validate the importance of solidarity, not just compliance. Over time, nurture fundamental motivations for sharing beyond prizes or praise. Help them tune into the joy that sharing brings.

Learning the Art of Turn-Taking

Alongside sharing, graciously taking turns allows all children to participate and builds patience. Turn-taking opens doors for compromise, so reinforce this habit. Taking turns teaches equitable distribution of resources—an important lesson.

Incorporate games that cue switching off turns, like Jenga, Hot Potato, or Follow the Leader dancing. Use visual timers like hourglasses to represent tangible waiting periods. Say, "When the sand runs out, we trade." Initially, keep turns brief for young ones' attention spans. If they lose interest, it means the turn length needs shortening.

Give turn transition prompts verbally, too. During activities, announce, "Sarah's turn is ending. Michael, you're next!" If they struggle with turn transitions, empathize first. "You want more time, I know. Here's a hug." Then, reorient them politely. Offer a warning as their turn wraps up so they can prepare mentally.

Resist impatiently seizing items from children when turns conclude. Instead, redirect, "This is Maya's toy now until the sand runs out. What can you play with in the meantime?" Then, praise cooperative transitions. "Thank you for sharing nicely!" Provide alternatives to bridge their waiting time.

With practice, prompt turn-taking generalizes to contexts like conversations or playground interactions. Notice your child waiting patiently for their turn and affirm it. The more frequently successes are highlighted, the more the motivation sticks. Gently nurture this interpersonal rhythm until it becomes second nature. Turn-taking creates the dance of smooth social functioning.

Cultivating Empathy in Children

Empathy provides emotional glue, allowing groups to bond. Model putting yourself in others' shoes so children gain intuitive practice. Start with empathy toward your child, seeking to understand their internal world. Demonstrate empathy skills through actions big and small. Greet neighbors warmly; thank cashiers sincerely. Notice those who may be marginalized around you. Discuss perspectives of book characters dealing with conflicts. When reading, ask, "How would you feel?" or "Why did they react that way?" Spot opportunities to cultivate compassion wherever you go. There are always hurting people who need understanding. Lead with empathy in all conversations and interactions.

Guide children to reflect on how words and behaviors impact others. If siblings argue, ask them gently later once they are calm, "How did your yelling make your sister feel?" Connect more dots about emotional impact. Role-play resolutions together. "What could you do instead next time and why?" The goal is to increase self-awareness, not shame them. We all have room for growth in understanding others' feelings. Meet them where they are developmentally. Use conflict as a teachable moment for building their capacity for empathy.

Read books exploring feelings and social dynamics. Select stories that expose compassionate concepts or cultural differences. Ask, "Have you ever felt like that character?" Foster discussion of emotions beyond the literal page at deeper levels. How did the story make you think differently about the experiences of others? With patience and wisdom, empathy grows into a way of deeply relating to all people. Seek out literature and media that expand their circle of care..

Building Cooperation Through Play

Cooperative play teaches vital interpersonal skills like communication, compromise, and bonding. Lead group activities emphasizing collaboration and collective problem-solving. Even competitive games like sports can build cooperative strategies. Teach them to balance cooperation and healthy competition.

Organize play dates for building projects. Gather neighborhood children for pretend ice cream shop startups requiring planning and teamwork. Foster leadership skills, too, by guiding them to coordinate roles. Enroll in sports teaching coordination like basketball, soccer, or doubles tennis. Support the coach's emphasis on teamwork. Ask coaches to highlight collaborative efforts, not just individual talents.

Spot children aligning peer interactions cooperatively in real-time. Narrate when you observe compromise and compassion. "Nice job taking turns even when you disagreed!" Reinforce flexibility when conflicts arise over roles or rules. Guide compromises if needed, then praise resolution. Highlight how they made progress working as a team. Encourage constructive dialogue in moments of conflict.

The more cooperative play gets prompted, the more cognitive pathways for successful collaboration solidify. What may start as guided play transforms into intrinsic habits of effective cooperation benefiting life relationships long-term. Keep sowing cooperative seeds. Teamwork will grow! These lessons become an ingrained social intelligence that carries through life.

Apply It! Creative Role Play

Let's practice our empathy, cooperation, and sharing skills through some imaginative role-play! This activity boosts creativity, too.

Gather costume pieces, props, and arts/crafts supplies from around the house. Then choose a scenario below or invent your own::

Sharing Shelter:

A big storm destroyed your community's houses so everyone must share one big shelter together. Figure out how to share space and resources.

Cooperative Meal:

You are all different animal characters working together to gather food and cook a meal to share with other animals.

Empathy Emergency!

A sad monster is feeling lonely and left out. Create and act out a way to respond with empathy and inclusion.

Instructions:

- Assign cooperative roles like prop creators, costume designers, cast members, etc.

- Gather materials, then build any items you'll need for the scene.

- Meet up and discuss what shared goals your characters have. How can empathy guide your story?

- Improvise! Act out your role-play scenario cooperatively.

- Afterward, reflect on how it went. What went well working together? Were there any struggles? How did you navigate them?

By immersing in fictional cooperative scenarios, we can rehearse the prosocial skills needed to tackle real-world challenges in the future! Use imagination along the way as an added bonus. So, let the dramatic role play begin!

Nurturing Social Skills

As we conclude this exploration of nurturing prosocial skills for rising generations, remember that foundations morph slowly but powerfully over time. The empathy modeled today becomes compassion shown tomorrow. Turn-taking expands into democratic dialogue and decision-making in communities. A willingness to share one's apple as a toddler may grow into the generosity of spirit that feeds the hungry someday.

Continue gently fostering the habits of giving, waiting, and understanding without demanding perfection or instant societal change. Consistency and compassion are key. Meet children where they struggle with egocentrism today, then lead them humbly toward more inclusive thinking bit by bit, year by year. For like the swelling tree, growth occurs through steady nourishment and care. May all you've read empower your family's journey toward more light.

Case Study: Cultivating Compassion

Zoe is a bright 7-year-old who excels academically yet struggles relating to peers. She tends to fixate on ensuring activities align with her preferences, growing upset when she can't select games or impatient when forced to share toys. Zoe's mother, Amanda, noticed that she rarely considers other children's feelings.

Wanting to nurture more empathy and cooperation long-term, Amanda turned to this chapter for guidance. She focused first on modeling inclusive language and behavior in their home to provide Zoe examples, saying things like "Here's a snack for you" before taking one herself. Amanda demonstrated turn-taking in conversations, assuring Zoe felt heard.

During play dates when conflicts arose over toy sharing, Amanda gently guided compromises, asking, "How can we take turns so both of you feel happy?" She resisted simply scolding Zoe but instead facilitated solutions teaching flexibility. Afterward, Amanda praised Zoe for listening and compromising, highlighting how sharing strengthened her friendship.

Amanda also planned structured activities intentionally exercising compassion, like cooperative art projects. She reinforced praising teamwork over individual outcomes. Before bedtime, Amanda chose picture books exploring the emotions and perspectives of characters dealing with interpersonal problems. She asked Zoe open questions like, "Why do you think her friend felt left out when she wasn't picked for the game?"

Over months of Amanda modeling empathy, enforcing turn-taking, and exploring social dynamics through literature, Zoe demonstrated increasing awareness of others' needs. Though still preferring control, she learned to share toys to sustain play dates longer. Zoe also contributed more actively during family discussions rather than only fixating on her own interests.

While still benefiting from practice, Zoe's emotional intelligence showed great promise. Amanda felt proud watching her consider new angles, understand different reactions based on background, and compromise more willingly when conflicts arose. The power of consistency modeling compassion bore fruit over time.

This case illustrates that while egocentrism dominates early childhood cognition, intentionally nurturing prosocial skills lays foundations. Consistent inclusion, empathy modeling, and scaffolding cooperation plants seeds allowing generosity to slowly take root if tended patiently.

Amanda also realized that these lessons extended beyond benefiting friendships. By learning to consider diverse perspectives, Zoe gained an appreciation for communities beyond her immediate circle. Her worldview expanded through stories depicting hardship and Amanda discussing those less fortunate. This cognitive shift toward more compassionate relating forged greater purpose and belonging.

Case Study: Building Camaraderie

Marco is a friendly yet competitive 10-year-old who thrives in individual sports like martial arts and track. Though sociable, he views team activities mostly as opportunities to showcase his athletic abilities. Marco fixates on personal statistics and awards, losing motivation if he's not the star player.

His coach, Vaughn, noticed that Marco struggled to collaborate, often excluding less skilled teammates by refusing to pass balls or dismissing their strategic input. Wanting to nurture more well-rounded leadership abilities in Marco, Vaughn turned to this chapter's tips on reinforcing cooperation and compromise.

He first modeled empathy himself by asking Marco's thoughts on plays, encouraging him to see different athletic roles as equally vital. Vaughn said things like, "Your quickness grabbing rebounds makes points possible for shooters downcourt!" to underscore interdependency.

Vaughn also restructured drills to require peer coordination, intentionally praising the process of aligning efforts, not just end-scoring results. He high-fived Marco for good passes that assisted team goals, reminding him, "Assists add up too!"

Additionally, Vaughn spotted Marco's natural mentoring instincts emerging occasionally when he coached struggling players during scrimmages. Vaughn immediately praised Marco for offering guidance, saying, "Thanks for showing Jim that technique. Your tips improved his game!"

When conflicts happened over positions or mistakes costing Marco's stats, Vaughn reinforced compassion. Once emotions cooled post-game, he facilitated reflectively, asking, "How do you think Noah felt being yelled at? What's your responsibility as a leader moving forward?" This prompted Marco to eventually apologize for his hurtful reactions.

Over the season, Vaughn nurtured Marco's teamwork mentality through modeling, reinforcement of process over outcomes, and reflective debriefs. Marco demonstrated noticeably more patience, assisting struggling athletes enthusiastically to lift group skill sets rather than fixating on personal glory.

This case study demonstrates that even independent high-achievers can broaden perspectives toward valuing camaraderie. By creatively structuring cooperation into competition, redirecting praise onto enabling others' success, and role modeling selfless behaviors, coaches cultivated Marco's leadership style from "me" to "we." Consistency nurturing collective growth over lone achievement paved the way for internalizing prosocial habits.

Vaughn also involved parents by briefing them on Marshall's collaborative progress and suggesting home opportunities to strengthen skills. He equipped Marco's parents to reinforce teamwork verbally while fostering empathy and compromise during sibling conflicts, too. This multidimensional support system accelerated Marshall's cooperative capacities exponentially.

Chapter Six

Chapter 6: Positive Role Modeling

They say actions speak louder than words. This rings profoundly true when it comes to raising children consciously through intentional modeling. Far more than what we preach, our children observe and absorb the behaviors, attitudes, communication styles, and problem-solving strategies we actually demonstrate daily. They integrate these lived values into their developing blueprints for relating with the world.

In the following pages, we will explore the incredible opportunity available through deliberately exemplifying emotional intelligence, conflict resolution, stress management, self-reflection, empathy, and responsibility in front of our little witnesses. When children have trusted role models embodying care, courage, and wisdom before their watchful eyes, seeds of greatness get planted within. Our example guides their blossoming.

The Power of Modeling Desired Behavior

Children are always observing and absorbing lessons from our actions—both positive and negative. That's why embodying the attitudes and behaviors we wish to cultivate in children serves an invaluable modeling function. Live what you want them to learn. Strive for consistency, living out core values like patience, honesty, cooperation, and compassion in front of children. How we communicate with a spouse when frustrated or treat a server at a restaurant makes a formative impression. Lead by example, handling challenges positively. Model under stress what you expect from them when they are under pressure.

Let children witness healthy conflict resolution firsthand when problem-solving with others. Demonstrate calm listening, validating multiple perspectives, and compromising respectfully. Avoid toxic communication patterns like shouting or contempt. Apologize if you slip into poor communication, then explain how you'll avoid that next time. Speaking gently, managing anger constructively, and resolving differences fairly in your home become the implicit curriculum for your little observers. Children integrate these interpersonal skills modeled by closely trusted adults at deep levels. Show them how it's done by living out examples. They will imitate your conflict strategies later with friends.

So be mindful of exemplifying your best self—they are taking notes! The behaviors and communication values you practice shape their developing minds perhaps even more than direct words alone. Consciously model patience and compassion. You are their first guru about how to handle emotions and relationships. Your example guides their journey immensely.

Demonstrating Healthy Stress Management

Children not only observe our positive behaviors but also how we handle hardship. Model resilient coping when you feel anxious, overwhelmed, or face dilemmas. Show them what to do with simmering inner tension rather than denial or explosion. Verbally walk through calming tactics out loud as you use them. "I'm feeling frustrated about this problem. I'm going to take some deep breaths first before responding." Demonstrate pressing pause on reactions, taking body-settling walks, talking feelings out with allies, etc. If you slip into poor coping, sincerely apologize afterward and explain what you'll try instead next time.

Likewise, tackle problems constructively in front of children. Break intimidating projects into doable chunks. Brainstorm multiple solutions rather than getting rigid. Be humble, asking mentors for help when needed. Show children how empowering that is rather than weak. Narrate your problem-solving process so they learn the skill. Also, explain when problems have no perfect solution but require compromise.

Staying calm in a crisis reassures children that challenges can be managed. Demonstrating self-composure combined with tactical problem-solving instills a "this too shall pass" confidence. It teaches that anxiety may visit but never has to stay. Our resilience provides their mental model for handling difficulty when it inevitably arises. In tough moments, remind them of times you persevered together before. You are their rock and guide for developing grit.

Modeling the Heart of Empathy

Beyond behaviors and coping strategies, our subtle attunement and respect toward others' emotional experiences also leave heavy impressions. Make empathy building a conscious priority in front of children. Start by deeply listening to your child's inner world with presence and care. Give full listening presence when family members express vulnerably. Thank them for sharing openly then ask clarifying questions to understand deeper layers. Validate their feelings by naming the emotions you sense. "That sounds really discouraging and lonely. I would feel sad, too." Teach that all emotions are welcome here.

Likewise, narrate your feelings and insights when dealing with interpersonal rifts. "I realize I really hurt her by those words. I didn't mean harm, but that doesn't erase her pain." Model self-review of impact on people different than you. Admit when bias clouded your understanding. Make repairs out loud so your children witness the process.

Exposing the anatomy of relationships and repairing disconnection requires courage. Demonstrate humility in reconciling cross-cultural conflicts. "Help me understand your tradition better, so I avoid ignorance going forward." Share stories of those facing hardship. How does privilege limit perspectives? What don't you see yet?

Children observe how valued people in their lives relate to those both similar and different. Are they open to growth or judging from assumptions? Do they get quiet or defensive during conflict? Your subtle heart-modeling teaches volumes through little moments accumulated over time. May it reflect expansive tolerance and care. You are their first window into courageous compassion.

Resolving Conflict in Healthy Ways

Disagreements and hurt are inevitable, even in close relationships. What matters most is how conflict gets handled when it emerges. Leverage moments of interpersonal tension as opportunities for modeling peaceful resolution. Remain calm when facing turmoil. Children take cues from your stability.

When arguing with a partner or family member, invite children to witness how you compromise respectfully. "I'm sorry for raising my voice earlier. Let's take 20 minutes to calm down and then discuss this rationally." Demonstrate reconciliation rituals like hugging to heal rifts quickly before bed. Reconnect even when apologies feel premature. Timeouts prevent escalation.

Teach that anger itself is not bad, but certain expressions of anger hurt others unnecessarily. Distinguish emotions from behaviors. "I understand you feel mad, but name-calling crosses a line." Then, redirect to healthy outlets like talking it out, journaling, or exercising to shift energy. Suppressing anger breeds resentment. Vent in constructive, not destructive, ways.

Guide children through altercations with siblings calmly. Help both verbalize their feelings using emotional vocabulary. Then facilitate compromise like taking turns or apologizing. Praise respectful conflict management, emphasizing the value of relationships above all. Remind them that you argue because you care. Anger signals investment in each other.

Model leveraging discord for growth in communication skills, self-awareness, and deeper bonds built through effort. Children observe not just what gets said but, more importantly, how we resolve matters of the heart. May they absorb wisdom carrying this forward. Conflict resolution is a skill continually refined over our lifetimes. We all remain students.

The Gift of Self-Reflection

Beyond concrete behaviors, regularly model life-long habits of contemplation and ownership regarding how your conduct impacts others—positively and negatively. Openly discuss thought processes prompting decisions big and small. "Here's what I was considering when responding to Aunt Lina that way..." Verbalize weighing moral dilemmas out loud. What gets sacrificed on either path? Who suffers unforeseen harm? Pose searching questions, then examine the options. Sleep on it before reacting if revelations prove uncomfortable. Ask your child what they would have done differently and why.

Just as important is revisiting and critiquing past behaviors out loud around children. Did impatience unintentionally demean someone? Insensitive words reveal lingering prejudice? Analyze how to make different choices moving ahead. Think through what triggers those behaviors.

Of course, admit mistakes outright when identified. "I really minimized your struggles earlier by saying to just get over it. I apologize. You deserve more compassion and listening from me when you're stressed." Own the misstep with clarity, then share lessons learned about blind spots. Also, explain how you'll avoid that in the future. Outline any repair work needed.

By unveiling internal reckoning and shouldering responsibility over time, you model integrity's maturation for children. The journey of progress contains missteps along the path, yet humility and courage guide us forward. We must keep each other accountable with love and wisdom.

Cultivating the Heart of Gratitude

Amidst the busyness of daily life, make thankfulness a constant companion, modeling openly appreciative attitudes for children to absorb.

Find abundant reasons for gratitude staring back at you. Start by being grateful for your child and voicing that often. Verbally recognize kindnesses from loved ones and strangers alike. Express genuine gratefulness for the child who shares a toy, the spouse who handles chores when exhausted, and the friend who lends a listening ear during grief. Write thank you notes detailing impacts made. Make a gratitude journal listing daily reasons for thanks.

Equally important, encourage children to voice appreciation, too. Have family members exchange gratitude. Prompt writing peer thank you cards at school. Weave gratitude into holiday traditions and mealtime rituals. Note acts of service community members provide. Show up with small tokens of thanks. Provide creative ideas for tangible expressions like drawings or cookies.

Seeds of entitlement grow quickly without vigilance. Nourish humility through consistent modeling that we all depend on others—and they on us in equal measure. Pay help forward when possible. Foster eyes that are attuned to unearned privilege and its impacts on human dignity. Discuss times you took kindness for granted. How can you reciprocate now?

Gratitude grounded in compassion greases the wheels of healthy relationships and just societies. Guide children in realizing the blessings already surrounding them and the power of paying blessings forward. We reap what we sow in visible and invisible ways. When gratitude flows freely, life feels less like bitterness and more like belonging.

Apply It! Family Role Play

Let's act out various family scenarios to practice demonstrating positive communication, empathy, problem-solving, and other social-emotional skills. This activity builds our modeling capacities in an engaging way!

Gather props like household items and costumes and print out the role-play scenario ideas below. Also, feel free to invent your own! Assign family members different roles. Discuss goals for the situation then begin the role play.

Possible scenarios:

- Resolving a sibling argument over a toy

- Dealing with disappointments or stressful events

- Expressing appreciation to each other

- Handling a mistake or conflict respectfully

- Communicating openly about a problem

- Supporting someone who is sad or worried

Take turns acting out family dynamics in both constructive and poor ways. Contrast what it looks like. Afterward, discuss what worked well and what could improve. Then, replay those scenarios, integrating that feedback.

Investing time in these rehearsals pays off by clarifying effective modeling strategies while infusing fun and creativity. We get to step into each other's shoes, building empathy and wisdom. Bonus perk: silly, memorable moments to look back on! Are you ready to role-play for learning?

It's the Little Things

As we conclude this chapter, remember that modeling happens through the micro-moments of everyday life, even more than grand speeches. Therefore, infuse intention into your subtle demonstrations of patience when a child gets frustrated by staying calm during conflicts and demonstrating responsibility by owning mistakes and modeling gratitude for people's kindness.

Your children's minds and hearts absorb the emotional strategies and moral processing you display outside classroom lectures. Model self-awareness and growth so they learn integrity's maturation over perfection. Demonstrate repairing injuries so they know that relationships can heal. Keep exemplifying compassion in the face of hardship, so they cultivate resilience when storms rage during their own journeys someday, too.

Your demonstration today becomes their intuition tomorrow. May all you model reflect your highest ideals—the goodness within will ripple outward for generations. Our children learn from our living light.

Case Study: Leading By Example

Camila is a 32-year-old teacher and mother of two children: Diego, age 6, and Maya, age 4. Having studied child psychology and experienced both positive and negative parental role models herself, Camila firmly believes in the power of intentional modeling for nurturing emotional intelligence and character development.

Camila demonstrates deliberately what she most wants to be embodied by her children: nonviolent conflict resolution, a growth mindset when facing challenges, responsibility, empathy, and optimism during hardship. Knowing children integrate modeled behaviors at deep levels, Camila aims to exemplify emotional regulation and interpersonal values in front of Diego and Maya daily.

For example, when the family faces disappointing news derailing vacation plans, Camila verbalizes resilience out loud. "This is sad, for sure. I was really looking forward to our trip, too. But focusing on solutions feels better than staying upset. Let's snuggle tonight, then brainstorm ideas tomorrow after a good rest." Her calm, paired with problem-solving, teaches her children that difficulty can be handled.

Camila also models self-awareness and integrity, owning personal mistakes that negatively impact others. After losing patience and yelling disrespectfully, she sincerely apologizes, outlining what she'll improve. Her humility and accountability demonstrate that no one is perfect, but everyone can grow wiser.

Knowing her reactions educate developing minds, Camila deliberately emphasizes forgiveness and compromise, practicing conflict resolution skills with her husband Javier openly. She demonstrates reconciling respectfully so Diego and Maya absorb blueprints for communicating through anger or hurt without attacking dignity.

Camila's children have come to mirror her steadiness in coping through events like pandemic unrest or financial challenges. They embody her creative optimism when facing setbacks and her tendency to respond with graciousness, not bitterness, toward interpersonal pains. Most pivotally, Camila has nurtured courage and resilience within them for life's ups and downs by deliberately modeling her best self even during storms.

This case study on Camila's family underscores the incredible influence caregivers wield through what they demonstrate before little witnesses daily, not just what they preach. Consciously exemplifying emotional regulation and moral values pays forward, profoundly shaping generations' destinies. Our steady modeling before young observers anchors their blossoming character.

Case Study: How Min Sets the Tone in His Blended Family

Min is a divorced father with 50/50 custody of his two sons: Aiden, age 8, and Caleb, age 6. Remarried to Sarah for three years now, they are nurturing bonds between all four family members, including Sarah's daughter Lily.

Min believes strongly in modeling to the children how healthy relationships function day-to-day. Having come from a fragmented family of origin himself, plagued by substance abuse and anger issues, he is determined to demonstrate security, maturity, and consistency for the next generation under his wing now.

Knowing children intuitively learn relationship blueprints from those closest to them, Min makes communication with Sarah a priority. He initiates weekly check-ins, assessing family emotional needs and strategizing any changes required. Min voices appreciation freely for Sarah's devotion to nurturing their crew. He also demonstrates humility by apologizing quickly if impatience or misunderstanding ever causes harm, then outlining how he will avoid repeating those dynamics.

During blended sibling conflicts, Min maintains calm while guiding collaborative compromise between upset parties. He resists disengaging emotionally or overfunctioning in rescue mode. Min provides balanced empathy for multiple perspectives while upholding boundaries of mutual respect. His reflexive hopefulness and conflict mediation skills model resilience despite each child processing this transition differently.

Over years of observing intimate glimpses of accountability, compassion through friction, and commitment to growth, the children have integrated emotional intelligence foundations for their own blossoming relationships. They readily employ his common language of feeling understood, avoiding assumptions, and repairing rifts through openness. Min has nurtured this blended family tree steadfastly like a wise gardener—protecting still-tender roots vulnerably intertwining while making space for each unique shape to stretch toward sunlight.

This case study demonstrates the subtle yet pivotal modeling parents provide regarding communication values, managing conflict, and nurturing emotional security. When caregivers exemplify integrity in navigating relationships at home, children receive visceral templates for relating with mindfulness, courage, and care throughout their own lives. Our steady demonstration becomes their intuition to carry forward.

Chapter Seven

Chapter 7: Conflict Resolution

Like gardeners nurturing young seeds, parents and teachers play a profound role in cultivating the conflict-resolution abilities of children. How we respond when disagreements inevitably arise models essential skills that blossom into lifelong competencies.

In the following pages, you will discover practical methods for teaching empathy, active listening, responsible self-expression, creative problem-solving, forgiveness, and apology. We'll cover sample dialogues and role-play activities, too. Consider each strategy as a gift toward equipping young hearts and minds to harvest harmony over hostility when facing interpersonal challenges today and for years beyond.

While conflict can never be avoided entirely, our influence gently shapes wiser choices, diminishing painful impacts. If we sow the seeds of compassionate communication and relationship repair early on, future generations may come to resolve differences through restored connection rather than escalating cycles of violence. Now, let us explore doing our small part.

Cultivating the Art of Listening

Beyond reflexively stating our side during conflicts, crucial communication skills like mindful listening and owning perspectives using "I" language can transform relationships. Guide children by practicing these tools. Teach that listening well requires tuning out internal distractions and focusing all attention on the speaker. We listen with more than just our ears.

First, set the stage for attentive listening by having children face speakers, offer eye contact, nod to show engagement, and briefly summarize content back. Teach that the goal is understanding others, not just preparing rebuttals. We listen to connect first. Check for accuracy in your paraphrasing. Did you fully capture their meaning? Seek to stand in their shoes.

Prompt "I" statements to express needs and feelings from the self versus blaming externally. For example, "I feel really sad when you use that nickname" instead of "You're so mean." Help children translate finger-pointing into taking personal responsibility. Speak from the heart. Discuss how "you" statements often trigger defensiveness, blocking mutual understanding.

Coach applying these tactics during family disagreements. When tensions emerge, initiate thoughtful pauses where each side listens and then reflects back what they heard. Follow that by having both restate viewpoints, starting sentences with "I." Finding common ground becomes more possible over time. With regular rehearsals, these skills become ingrained habits benefiting all relationships long-term.

Patiently nurturing, mindful, compassionate communication rituals plants seeds, improving relationship health for years. Even when conflict continues, bonds strengthen through feeling genuinely heard, understood, and cared for despite differences. That connection anchors us. Communication largely determines the health of our emotional ecosystems.

Mastering Healthy Self-Expression

Unresolved emotions simmering beneath surface conflicts often fuel aggression or retreat. Teach children to articulate feelings constructively instead. Start by listening compassionately as they express upsets to model safe vulnerability. Start by expanding their emotional vocabulary through listening, literature, and discussion around experiences. When upset, prompt them to name the sensations and roots beyond "good/bad." Guide them to speaking feelings aloud, first to trusted allies, then eventually to the source of tension. You can use charts and word lists to teach and broaden their awareness of feelings.

Share communication techniques like owning perspectives with "I" language versus blaming others. Also, explain how volume or intensity can intimidate. Encourage assertiveness using respectful words, tone, and body language. Role play to practice. Praise effort toward healthy expression. Growth takes repetition without judgment. Provide peaceful communication tips to defuse rising tensions.

As children gain skills identifying and modulating inner states, immediately explosive reactions become replaced with emotional awareness. Channel the wisdom, then guide appropriate behavioral responses. Progress unfolds gradually, so remain patient. Meet them where they are developmentally and stretch skills further over time through compassionate coaching.

Creative Conflict Resolution

When disagreements emerge, sideline unproductive blame to focus on solutions. Guide children through a process of creative reconciliation. Approach tension as an opportunity for growth.

Train attention on defining the core problem neutrally, respecting all sides. Use "I" statements to explain personal concerns. Then collaboratively brainstorm a menu of potential resolutions without critique. Affirm creative ideas first. Ensure all voices get heard during the brainstorming.

Next, evaluate options together, considering fairness, sincerity, and relationship repair. Discuss likely outcomes from compassionate listening, apologies, compromise, or resetting expectations on both sides. Choose reasonable paths forward through consensus. Also, discuss why proposed solutions may not work well as part of the learning.

Over time, this intentional process promoting cooperation beyond compliance yields more harmony. Children gain confidence in navigating conflict through goodwill, courageous communication, and commitment to mutual understanding. Revisit what worked and what requires refinement to improve next time.

The Healing Power of Forgiveness

No matter how close, conflict inevitably injures relationships now and then. What matters most is how amends get made long-term through sincere apologies, letting go, and rebuilding trust. Meet tensions with empathy, insight, and maturity.

When encouraging apologies after wrongdoing, ensure that words reflect genuine remorse and responsibility rather than just obligatory

RAISING EMOTIONALLY HEALTHY CHILDREN IN... 91

platitudes. Discuss true repentance requiring changed actions, not just speech. Also, explain that forgiveness is a gift that is not guaranteed.

Equally pivotal, help children understand that forgiveness is its own gift, extending grace to others after pain. Vent feelings but also recognize humanity's shared fallibility. "I forgive but won't forget" keeps us guarded versus renewed through releasing anger. Breathe life slowly back into connection. Forgiveness fosters emotional and spiritual health when anger no longer consumes.

There will always be moments of friction. Yet the manner in which injuries get cleaned and bound afterward determines whether affection continues sharing life's journey in deeper ways going forward. Help children have the courage to mend. Time alone does not heal wounds. Intention and care do.

Learning Through Dramatic Play

While discussing conflict resolution tactics is useful, children better integrate skills through hands-on rehearsal. Tap into their power of imagination and dramatic role-play to create insight and empathy.

Craft simple puppets together or gather props reflecting diverse personalities and scenarios. Then, act out interpersonal disputes from playground drama to peer pressure situations. Explore hurtful events from multiple angles. "What might they each feel and need?" Promote speaking openly in play mode first.

Guide by reenacting escalations, then model healthier responses like "I" language, apologizing, or walking away respectfully. Contrast against poor communication like dismissiveness, insults, or violence. Discuss takeaways afterward. What behaviors worsen disputes? Which skills effectively defused tensions?

When children repeatedly practice peaceful conflict management within creative scenarios, neural pathways solidify, making wiser choices second nature when real relationship challenges later arise. An added perk: Laughter and bonding build resilience to approach discord more calmly. Turn tension into playful growth through role play.

Apply It! Creative Conflict Resolution Role Plays

Practicing conflict management skills through various role-play scenarios boosts real-world application. Let's brainstorm imaginary conflicts and resolutions together!

Supplies: Craft materials like cardboard, fabric, paper-mâché to make masks, props, or puppets, costume items, and household stuff representing locations. Print the role-play prompts below.

1. Make simple puppets/masks/props together to represent story characters and places.

2. Choose a conflict scenario idea or invent your own. Discuss possible constructive responses.

3. Act out escalations using unhealthy communication like yelling. Pause and discuss impacts.

4. Model healthier conflict management like empathy, apology, and compromise. Try multiple endings!

5. From the role play, contrast scenarios, noting what behaviors worsened or solved tensions.

Scenarios:
- Friends arguing over which game to play

- Sibling took a toy without asking
- Someone feeling left out of friend group
- Being pressured unfairly by peers
- Parent and child upset over chores/responsibilities

Through dramatic rehearsal, we can playfully gain confidence in navigating real disagreements in wiser ways. In addition, creativity sparks fun bonding! What imaginative conflict-diffusing ideas can you add?

Peaceful Resolutions

As we conclude, equipped with abundant concepts and tools for conflict transformation, take comfort in knowing that long-term progress unfolds through small steps. Simply modeling one new communication ritual or coaching empathetic perspective-taking through a story plants fertile seeds. Build on strengths already emerging.

Walk the path with patience, playfulness, and care. Children integrate lessons best through consistent living examples versus formal lectures alone. Tend the garden daily through your demonstrations of forgiveness, responsibility, and nonviolent expression. Core skills take years to blossom. But what we nurture today lays the groundwork for more peaceable children to grow into adults who heal divides instead of fueling them. Now let us till hopeful soil together.

Case Study: Cultivating Communication

Zane is a bright yet strong-willed 10-year-old who argues frequently with his parents and teachers when receiving feedback perceived as criticism. Rather than accept responsibility for poor grades or behavioral issues, he reflexively denies, makes excuses, and points blame elsewhere. Zane's defensiveness exasperates adults trying to guide him.

His school counselor recognized that Zane lacked essential conflict resolution communication tools like reflective listening and "I feel" statements. She suggested Zane's parents nurture perspective-taking and self-expression abilities using techniques from this chapter.

Zane's mother, Aisha, made efforts to model vulnerable sharing of feelings when tensions emerged over missed homework or chores. Rather than reactive scolding, she used "I" statements to take ownership of the impacts of his irresponsible actions. Aisha also practiced reflective listening, summarizing Zane's deflections and reframing them into actionable needs.

Gradually, through Aisha's demonstrations, Zane learned to identify the roots of discomfort himself using emotional vocabulary. Coached to express upset directly rather than project it outward onto others, Zane grew more receptive to hearing how his behaviors affect family members without instantly denying feedback.

Aisha also role-played common tension scenarios with Zane, like receiving critical input from a coach or confronting friends during conflicts. She modeled self-restraint, hearing both sides while also making space for Zane to assert his viewpoint respectfully. Through pretend scenarios, Zane rehearsed taking responsibility, compromising, and apologizing for his part in disputes.

After months of Aisha and teachers patiently helping Zane articulate frustrations constructively and truly listen for understanding when problems arose, his knee-jerk reactive mode softened remarkably. Zane increasingly demonstrated skill in owning his role in the conflicts without deflecting blame elsewhere. Though still benefiting from skill-building, Zane's emotional intelligence and communication competence showed immense growth thanks to compassionate coaching.

This story demonstrates that by nurturing conflict management abilities like self-expression, empathy, and nondefensive listening, children's character and relationships stand to blossom beautifully over time. With caring cultivation, fiery seeds calm into wise, self-possessed communicators.

Case Study: Repairing Rifts

Camila teaches a lively fifth-grade class where interpersonal drama and conflicts frequently arise. Wanting to nurture essential emotional intelligence abilities in her students, Camila deliberately utilizes techniques from this chapter like facilitating forgiveness and compromise between feuding peers.

When two gifted yet competitive girls, Jade and Natalia, became locked in ongoing hostility sabotaging group work, Camila intervened by having them express their feelings through written letters. This allowed each girl to vent anger but also pushed reflective listening since they were required to paraphrase back the other's viewpoint before responding. Camila prompted them to incorporate "I feel" statements, owning their perspectives.

After mutual hurt surfaced into the open through the letters, Camila had girls imagine reconciling if they were longtime adult friends looking back with maturity. She asked, "What would strengthen your bond moving forward?" This visioning practice cultivated empathy while spotlighting how treasured connections suffer when grudges persist.

The complex reconciliation process prompted deep sharing only possible through Camila's compassionate moderation and consistency in upholding resolution. But soon, empathy emerged, allowing the feuding pair to acknowledge mutual fault and find forgiveness. Their academic collaboration and camaraderie were restored beautifully after learning these hard interpersonal lessons when young.

In another display of essential emotional skills, class clown Marco frequently interrupted lessons, provoking easy laughs from peers needing attention. Rather than reactive scolding, which could humiliate him, Camila used the technique of creative imaginary enactment from this chapter. At a later time, she had Marco dramatize the same class disruption in a corporate setting. This theatrical framing allowed Marco to witness unproductive aspects of his behavior from an outside lens. The class explored alternate positive ways he could gain peer belonging without disrupting group functioning. Marco's interruptions transformed into using his natural humor to facilitate learning through playful review games going forward!

Both vignettes reinforce how compassionately upholding relationship repair, creative re-framing of conflicts, and outlining useful alternatives allow children to evolve unproductive patterns into prosocial bonding. With a dedication to nurturing communication and forgiveness, divisions turn into lessons on nourishing community.

Chapter Eight

Chapter 8: Helping Your Child Overcome Obstacles in Life

During the storms of life, it is our desire to shield children from these events, but inevitably, the winds will blow and shake within their developing hearts and minds. Although adversity leaves an impact, it does not mean trauma will define who they are or block their destiny. Their resilience only requires activation.

In the following pages, you will discover how establishing safe harbors and consistent connections lays the foundations for children to unpack challenges nonjudgmentally. We'll explore modeling healthy coping strategies that process emotions constructively rather than ignoring or squashing them. You'll also find guidance on instilling growth mindsets, refusing to let wounds limit potential or painful pasts dictate futures.

Healing from hardship rarely follows formulas or timelines. However, seasons change. With patient cultivation of courage, vulnerability, and self-belief taking root through unconditional support, our children can grow stronger yet wiser from the storms that once battered them. Now, let us explore the path together.

No parent wants to see their child suffer. Yet hardship inevitably arises along the winding path of growth—whether in the form of bullying, loss, discrimination, or other trauma. The pain cuts deeply. However, the manner in which children respond often depends on the modeling and support received. Their circumstances need not define them. There is light ahead if allies walk beside them through the shadows.

Creating Safe Environments

First and foremost, children require physically and emotionally safe spaces to begin opening up about difficult experiences. Make home a secure base where judgment gets left at the door. Listen more than lecture. Emphasize understanding over problem-solving. Let them guide the pace, trusting you will handle their feelings with care. Model unconditional love.

It takes courage for children to unpack emotional burdens, especially with caregivers. Set aside distractions and be fully present when they start to share. Offer patience, not timelines. See past the behavior to the hurting heart within. With consistent vulnerability matched by consistent compassion in response, trust deepens bit by bit.

The Gift of Consistency

In the midst of turmoil, consistent family routines provide children with islands of refuge. Set regular schedules for sleeping, eating, playing, and learning balanced with fluid flexibility when needed. During parent conflicts, establish ceasefire rules shielding children from crossfire. Children gain confidence in facing external chaos when their inner worlds reflect relative peace. Guide them gently there.

When it comes to adversity, certainty rarely exists. Yet the reassuring certainty of your unwavering support makes space for children to process uncertainty. Establish reliable rituals like weekly check-ins, regular shared meals, and family meetings to update changing needs. Sameness forms solid ground beneath unstable footing when the world feels topsy-turvy. Security originates from within caring connections that are built to last.

Cultivating Coping Skills

Teach children healthy mechanisms for managing difficult emotions and releasing tension. The mythical "get over it" admonishments we once swallowed often only drive pain underground to resurface later. Demonstrate proactive self-care instead—modes of coping like journaling, exercise, deep breathing, or mindfulness techniques. Discuss thinking traps that worsen distress. Equip their toolbox with wisdom.

Have children list healthy versus unhealthy coping strategies. Which ones functionally address the root of frustration versus just masking symptoms? Help them expand emotional intelligence, recognizing that acting out often indicates a lack of self-regulation skills, not inherent flaws within a child. Guide them in speaking feelings and then channeling through suitable outlets like physical activities, creative expression, or focused breathing. Growth takes exploration.

Growth Mindsets Trump Limiting Labels

While professional support plays a pivotal role when adversity causes lasting impact, take care not to let victimhood permanently define a child's identity either. Counter limiting narratives children tell themselves about being too "broken" or "damaged" to heal. Challenge self-blame. Affirm untapped inner reservoirs of courage and resilience. There is no such thing as a lost cause—only lost patience from those who surrendered hope.

Discuss how we all have parts that feel broken sometimes. Explain common childhood misconceptions like assuming they caused divorces or abuse. Make space for vulnerability and tears. Share stories of those who overcame paralyzing pain to rediscover purpose, from Joanne Rowling to Viktor Frankl. Help reframe old wounds as wisdom. The most empowering words anyone hears may be those that first make children believe in themselves. Speak those words.

It may take sustained effort over months or years. Yet great oaks verdant with life grow precisely from what tried crushing them—the hardened knots and cracks once inflicted by heavy stones over seasons now transformed into the wood's strongest parts, never to be broken again. Our children can emerge the same, but only if we walk faithfully by their side, providing light until they stand tall on their own once more.

Apply It! Visualizing the Future

When hardship hits, it's easy to get stuck dwelling on the past or consumed by the pain of present challenges. This activity helps children look ahead positively, envisioning their futures.

Gather art supplies like paper, markers, and magazines to cut out. Have children complete the below prompts creatively:

- Envision your life 10 years from now as a young adult. Where are you living? Describe your home.

- What work or education are you engaged in? What skills have you gained?

- What relationships enrich your life? Describe activities done together.

- What hobbies or passions bring you joy day to day? How do you spend your free time?

- How have you grown on personal fronts like confidence, resilience, and wisdom? What challenges did you overcome?

- Guide children in creating visual representations of their future lives reflecting areas like career, connections, and growth. Have them share visions while you actively listen. Discuss dreams and strengths that emerged.

The act of imagining a bright tomorrow full of purpose seeds hope, powerfully countering trauma's crushing effect in the present. Picturing fulfilling potential paths ahead grounds children in larger processes of growth happening even amidst grief. Creative expression also relieves emotional buildup constructively. This simple exercise illuminates light awaiting beyond shadows.

Empowered People Empower Others

As we conclude this chapter on empowering children to overcome adversity, recall that your compassionate presence conveys far more than any particular strategy alone ever could. While practical guidance provides a roadmap, what children most require during periods of difficulty or darkness is a trusted companion reassuring them the sun still exists beyond overcast skies.

Believe boldly in their ability to heal and remind them of this belief frequently when doubt clouds their weary eyes. We need only nurture the strength already inside seeking release. When words seem inadequate, let your embrace speak volumes. For at the end of the day, love radiates warmth, drying tears shed from youthful faces gazing up, searching to know that they will be okay. Your unconditional love declares that they will. With this light to guide, the rest simply represents the journey.

Case Study: Rebuilding Hope

Samantha is a shy eighth grader who has suffered intense bullying by a group of peers for two years. The unrelenting exclusion and hurtful remarks resulted in Samantha sinking into a depression with plummeting self-esteem and frequent suicidal thoughts. She viewed herself as irreparably damaged after this trauma.

However, Samantha's parents, Ruth and Miguel, worked closely with school counselors and therapists, employing tactics from this chapter to nurture their daughter's mental health and resilience. They surrounded Samantha with unconditional love while providing tools to process the trauma without judgment.

Ruth made home a safe haven for the vulnerable processing of emotions tied to this crushing bullying. She supported Samantha in expressing pain through journaling and art, then reinforced strengths, noticing the courage it took to open up. Ruth frequently reminded Samantha that she was so much more than limiting labels bullies tried imposing.

Miguel signed them up for a peer support group helping those overcoming adversity. Hearing stories of others thriving despite discrimination nurtured hope during Samantha's darkest moments of doubting her future. The group also reduced the isolation trauma can breed.

By combating Samantha's skewed self-narratives, repeating she was too worthless or different to make friends, Ruth and Miguel gradually helped restore realistic perspective about her lovability. Their consistency in conveying unconditional pride and belief in her resilience over the years provided a secure base for facing her inner demons.

While much work remains to rebuild self-confidence, today, Samantha is embracing her passions for photography and poetry. She speaks about bullying prevention and supporting younger students and can now look back with maturity at enemies who will not dictate her identity or potential going forward.

This case study reinforces that with patient nurturance of coping abilities combined with caregivers combating limiting trauma narratives, young people can reclaim their sense of purpose and self-belief. Samantha's story proves that our light always outshines darkness if given compassionate fuel to ignite our inner torch once again.

Case Study: Miles' Metamorphosis

Miles is a sensitive boy who endured intense bullying throughout elementary school due to his learning disability and awkward social anxiety. Classmates teased Miles relentlessly, often escalating to physical aggression on the playground. Too paralyzed to tell teachers, Miles withdrew further into his shell.

At home, his parents, Jenny and Noah, noticed rising despondency. Miles fixated on self-hate, calling himself "stupid" and "pathetic." He adamantly resisted their encouragement, insisting he was too fundamentally flawed to make friends or succeed in life.

Jenny responded compassionately as Miles opened up about the bullying horrors. She asked how she could best support him emotionally. Together they listed adults like the principal or counselor whom Miles felt ready to disclose details for intervention development. Jenny role-played with Miles to rehearse assertive reporting until he felt more confident.

Noah also took Miles to meet a support group of learning-disabled teenagers, authors, and advocates who shared stories of hardship that ultimately transformed into purpose. Witnessing others like him who found belonging, career success, and tools for shame reduction instilled kernels of hope within Miles' resignation. The visualization activity in this chapter strengthened his envisioning of his own empowered future, too.

While not an instantly linear trajectory, Miles' parents' consistent emotional mirroring, distress tolerance modeling, and refusal to let trauma dictate potential slowly nurtured inner resilience and self-belief. Over the next decade, with ongoing scaffolding, Miles increasingly embraced his unique neurology through passions like inventing assistive technologies, poetry, and peer mentoring.

Today, Miles speaks proudly to groups of disabled students about overcoming bullying through self-advocacy. He discusses tuning out denigrating noise while unlocking talents society too narrowly measures. Miles blossomed beautifully from the fragile, defeated child he once saw reflected back in shame. His metamorphosis emerged through compassionately cultivating the seeds of resilience and voice when Miles felt silenced.

This powerful account demonstrates how meeting children at their points of pain with unconditional support combating limiting narratives can profoundly restore hope and strength over time. Our light cannot be extinguished without consent. Miles' story proves that even the most traumatized souls can reclaim their inner radiance when allies walk faithfully alongside, offering torches leading out from the darkness.

Chapter Nine

Chapter 9: Fostering Independence and Responsibility

As parents, one of our greatest yet bittersweet duties is nurturing children's independence so they can tackle life solo someday. We aim to shift from constant caregiver to consultant trusted for guidance when sought. What are nurturing steps to help children increasingly self-govern while avoiding premature freedom or rescue from consequences that foster irresponsibility? This chapter explores that gradual tango between steadfast support and high expectations, urging emerging young adults further up Maslow's hierarchy toward realizing their best selves.

Acquiring Essential Life Skills

Before launching children into adulthood, equip their toolkit with practical life competencies they will need once out of your nest through modeling and then measured mastery. Coach nutritious cooking basics, maintaining tidy living spaces devoid of endless clutter signaling inner chaos most often mirrored outwardly, and managing finances judiciously. Pass on survival skills like paying bills on time, resolving insurance issues, and gaining basic vehicle/home repair skills. Have teens file taxes yearly themselves with your oversight to demystify the process. Help them open checking/savings accounts to comprehend budgeting fully. Assign rotating household maintenance duties and teach teamwork, too. Resist hostage thinking, making you an indispensable martyr tied to tasks they must gradually own. Sure, inept attempts will exasperate, and things may get damaged, but how else will fledglings ever fly successfully solo? Patience and forgiveness help you and them progress together.

Also, carve out opportunities for failure-proofing during childhood, allowing small missteps to inoculate against catastrophe later when stakes intensify. Let an 8-year-old bake cookies solo as you observe quietly, even if extra salt gets dumped in unwisely. Have a tween assemble their bike, assuming instructions get followed, but merely guide if wheels start being installed backward. It's through these little laboratories of independent exploration they learn self-trust. Review gently afterward, then celebrate progress. Early freedom develops intuition and competence for when teenage autonomy arrives with cars, college, or finances needing to be handled alone.

Goal-Setting

and Planning

Beyond isolated skills, developing entire mindsets of diligence and determination helps children create lives not limited by current circumstances. Guide them in handwriting yearly goals each January, then chunk them into monthly and weekly action plans. Teach concepts like accountability partners, progress metrics, flexibility, reassessing paths, and pivoting from poor results quickly without shame. Have them journal frustrations when efforts fall short, then rewrite empowering interpretations focusing on self-improvement. Urge abandoning victim mentalities blinding them from seeing how much power resides within to produce change. Demonstrate taking responsible risks yourself, like new vocations attempted after career stagnation. Show them how those owning both contributions and consequences to outcomes thrive, whether stemming from initiative or errors. Permission to fail spectacularly liberates daring greatly.

Also, nurture self-awareness around tendencies sabotaging goal progress through avoidance, distraction, or self-pity. Have children diagnose their own pitfalls, gather tools addressing them, and then track improvement. If procrastination plagues, assign mini-objectives due every 48 hours. If concentration drifts, remove social media apps temporarily. If confidence crumbles, list previous wins. Guide them by positively reframing setbacks as necessary stepping stones. The goal is cultivating durable, flexible mindsets, persisting despite adversity, and not demanding perfection. Internal resilience and grit prepare them for adulthood's inevitable storms. Are we nurturing conviction or compliance? Inner direction or outer puppetry? Coherent character surpasses what credentials alone produce long-term.

Natural Consequences and Decision-Making

While collaborative authority helps shepherd children's growth at young ages, progress requires gradually transferring steering wheels into their hands fully. Guide but don't endlessly rescue, allowing discomfort from poor judgments to motivate wiser discernment henceforth naturally. After reasonable warnings, let children skip friends' birthdays without delivering forgotten gifts left home by distracted parents chronically living hectic reactionary existences. When irresponsible teenage drivers scrape cars or don't refill gas tanks promptly, require covering repair costs using their savings. Implement household contribution systems deducting expenses or granting rewards based on helpfulness. Logic outweighs lengthier lectures, and empathy prevents harshness. Yet accountability teaches that life often hands individuals back what energy and priorities they invest. Adulthood reality hits walls eventually if measures excessively cushion shortsightedness. Allow small failures now to build children's wisdom in managing much larger matters ahead independently.

Also, avoid accusations, shaming, or vindictive "I told you so" jabs, which often foster secrecy, not transparency, moving forward after missteps. Children still require guidance processing emotions around consequences without added burden from disappointed caregivers. Discuss what went awry conversationally, then redirect to potential remedies and lessons absorbed. When your warnings prove correct, it is time for humility, not superiority. Ask, "How can I support differently next time?" Resistance melts faster when receiving empathy, and self-trust strengthens when parents believe in children's abilities to self-correct, not just comply resentfully short-term. The goal is to lovingly mentor better discernment, not indict character. Wisdom awakens through patience with the process.

Incentivizing Responsibility

While idealistic reality insists that true integrity gets cultivated internally, insufficient motivation and undeveloped frontal lobes still need an external push. Early token economies provide transitional bridges toward more intrinsically driven responsibility. Set up charts where children earn play money redeemable for privileges when household duties are accomplished timely without nagging. Create bonus systems allowing later weekend curfews for every "A" gained that quarter. This incentivizes initial repetitions, establishing positive habits and neural pathways that increasingly self-propel. Always highlight how others benefit from their contributions too—family, teams, community. Use verbal praise abundantly to help kindheartedness sink deeper than surface actions alone. Arrange milestone celebrations for sustaining consistency as motivation wanes periodically from being overwhelmed or distracted. Inspire their greatest selves to keep seeking nobler paths.

Gradually shift praise from behavior compliance to intrinsic moral maturity. Name kindnesses they initiate unprompted or responsibilities upheld even when they think no one is looking. Reinforce self-discipline, not just external conformity. Wean token economies to underscore natural rewards like satisfaction gained through completion. With development, questioning replaces commands given. "Why is this task/value important even beyond incentives or penalties?" Push children to own rules rather than passively obey because authority positions dictate they must. Longitudinal studies reveal this fosters generativity and civic engagement in communities later as young adults. When children shift from "what will I get" to "who will I help" thinking, society profits exponentially.

Apply It! Goal Setting for Growing Responsibility

Let's set some SMART goals together focused on building important life skills and responsible habits!

SMART stands for:

Specific, Measurable, Achievable, Relevant, Time-bound

Grab a notebook to write down goals and action plans. Identify 1-3 skill areas needing improvement, like chore completion, homework diligence, or bedtime routine. Then use the template below:

Skill Chosen: Chore completion

Goal: Clear dinner dishes without reminders four times this week.

Plan: Set a phone alarm at the start of the meal to remember afterward. Post the chart listing days to check off.

Skill Chosen:

Goal:

Plan:

Now, choose appropriate rewards if goals are achieved, like a favorite meal cooked, movie night, extended curfew, etc. Make sure to celebrate progress!

When done, post these goal sheets visibly to stay motivated. Revisit and reset together weekly. Over time, notice your growing independence muscle helping tackle bigger goals ahead!

For even more impact, create collaborative goals with a parent or sibling focusing on household contributions, too. Hearing their perspectives, listening openly, and compromising to find solutions everyone feels good about builds maturity fast while strengthening family bonds. This interdependence allows independence to grow in healthy ways!

The Dances of Letting Go

Fostering independence resembles a marathon more than a sprint, as children's capacities ebb and flow. But each small step prepares their feet for adulthood's roads ahead nonetheless. Applaud effort and ethics more than outcomes, which often keep maturing as experience builds wisdom. Always keep in mind that their journeys are unfolding on your watch. Guide firmly when necessary but increasingly release controls where appropriate, always positioning your primary role as their steadfast safe harbor amidst storms, not the latest squall they face. Growth requires braving elements that strengthen resolve and self-trust. Soon, the apron strings you loosen form soft runways as fledglings soar toward awaiting horizons. Your job is simply opening cage doors wider—they will know instinctively when they are ready to fly free.

Case Study: Spreading Her Wings

Ever since her childhood, Julie's mom, Maria, tended to be overprotective about potential dangers, whether warning Julie obsessively when riding her bike around their quiet neighborhood or triple checking homework to prevent any missed assignments. Maria also routinely called Julie's college professors when grades concerned her, often without Julie's awareness or consent, despite Julie performing strongly overall.

However, when Julie entered her final undergraduate year, she met with Maria, explaining that she needed space to make her own choices—even if imperfect at times—so she could practice critical adult responsibility before graduation. Julie understood that Maria's worried protection stemmed from deep love, but she feared lacking the competence to handle life's curveballs ahead since Maria hadn't allowed small stumbles that teach grit throughout earlier years.

Maria recognized the truth in Julie's loving honesty. She agreed it was time to loosen the cords for Julie's self-assurance to keep maturing. Together, they discussed reasonable boundaries around academic oversight, noting what information Maria still required as a tuition contributor versus overstepping the autonomy that Julie deserved by determining her own priorities about projects or social events. Maria also promised to give Julie initial space to self-correct any minor missteps about things like oversleeping for an exam, only intervening if larger concerns like health or safety arose, warranting partnered problem-solving.

Additionally, Maria guided Julie in opening her first independent credit card to master financial responsibility through budgeting and earning rewards when possible versus accruing debt irresponsibly. This step held symbolic weight for Julie embarking on adult fiscal management.

Of course, the road toward complete self-sufficiency held challenges at times. But Maria nurtured supportive check-ins, not shaming criticism if Julie made mistakes like overdrawing her account or struggling to wake with alarms. Their rapport focused on processing lessons learned and creating plans to prevent repeats, but with accountability falling rightly upon Julie's shoulders.

Through respectful compromise that balances gentle guidance with growing autonomy, Julie not only succeeded in meeting graduation milestones independently but also felt prepared to embrace new adulthood adventures ahead with her inner compass reliably directing her onward.

Case Study: Letting Go with Love

As the single father of Marco, a bright yet strong-willed 8th grader, Sam walked a tightrope straddling involvement and independence with his son. They shared a close bond, yet Sam knew the coming high school years required gradually transferring responsibility to Marco in preparation for college and adulthood.

Sam decided to start by teaching Marco essential household life skills like doing laundry, preparing basic recipes, following budgets, and maintaining his living environment responsibly. Sam created checklists of age-appropriate tasks, explaining the importance of contributing to family functioning. He presented these new expectations warmly but firmly, emphasizing growth over punishment if Marco failed to uphold chores.

Additionally, when Marco protested losing tech privileges after breaking rules, Sam held calm boundaries, following through on reasonable consequences. He reminded Marco that integrity meant honoring commitments while explaining how trust and autonomy connect to accountability. Marco's complaints softened, realizing that violations jeopardized recently earned freedoms.

However, Sam balanced limit-setting with collaborative leadership, too—involving Marco in some family decisions like vacation plans or new household systems. Sam guided Marco through a goal-setting worksheet for this coming school year as well, urging Marco to consider skills he hoped to accomplish. Sam promised to support Marco's ambitions as an advisor while letting him increasingly self-direct.

Of course, the path toward independence hit bumps for both father and son. Marco's mistakes or forgetfulness exhausted Sam's patience at times. Heavy course loads overwhelmed Marco in the rigorous International Baccalaureate program. Yet Sam offered empathy versus lecturing during their frequent check-ins, analyzing what derailed progress and jointly strategizing solutions.

Although still a work in progress, Marco tackles this challenging curriculum and manages his schedule fairly independently today. He advocates needs without entitlement and responsibly balances school, friends, and self-care while contributing substantially to family stability. The consistent trust in his competence combined with accountability for missteps nurtured inner resilience and maturity to stand strong. Marco still relies on Dad's wisdom but finds confidence within to steer his expanding life wisely.

Chapter Ten

Chapter 10: Navigating the Digital Age Consciously

Few can deny technology's profound grip on society. Yet devices claiming to "connect us" often ironically disconnect users from present-moment awareness and real relationships tied to mental health. While useful in moderation, excessive or mindless screen time breeds anxiety in youth already wired to seek peer validation. How can we teach balance and restraining overindulgence? This chapter explores setting healthy boundaries and modeling intention over impulsion when engaging in the virtual world.

Establishing Media Rules and Limits

In order to successfully support our children, we need to proactively inform household media rules.

- Define device-free zones like bedrooms and mealtimes.

- Set up charging stations outside bedrooms overnight to prevent distraction.

- Utilize parental controls, allowing monitoring and time limits that encourage actual parenting again, not outsourcing.

- Require earbuds for gaming and apps so ambient noise doesn't overwhelm family members needing quiet.

- Ban devices for ages under two given critical brain development required and research confirming that usage offers no cognitive advantage this young anyway.

- Form print and digital media budgets for older children mirroring real-world financial literacy.

- Require balancing screen activities with reading, nature walks, household contributions, and self-care like sleep, nutrition, and exercise.

Our duty is to parent our children directly, not the digital clones we allow to consume reality for hours unattended.

Also, commit to understanding the digital landscape's allure before rigidly rejecting its tools. Attend a gaming tournament, ask about their favorite influencers, and learn the apps that absorb their spontaneous moments. By bridging generational differences, you regain influence. Neutrality builds trust to steer use versus becoming an obstacle to be tuned out. Discuss online content together to model critical thinking. Children benefit when mentors interpret modern phenomena thoughtfully, not fearfully. Stay curious.

Promoting Online Safety

Before unleashing teens to social media, discuss potential bullying, sexting coercion, depression from comparisons, or strangers exploiting naivety about privacy controls. Monitor interactions vigilantly since teens underestimate risks in the virtual playground. Share wisdom gained from past errors navigating digital territory so they avoid similar pitfalls. Ensure children know that removing or reporting online content barely diminishes reach once unleashed, so restraint protects reputations and mental health. Teach them that showing personality online differs considerably from demonstrating sound character offline earned through sacrifice, courage, and service. Emphasize that convention followers wield little influence compared with unconventional trailblazers shaping culture. Inspire their activism and artistry more than their "insta-image" fixation.

Also, instill ethics about proper technology usage, not just personal security. Discuss the dangers of anonymous vitriol that youth unwittingly perpetuate themselves on public platforms when emotions impulsively erupt. Guide children to pause before posting reactions. Model reconciliation habits online aligned with off-line values when conflicts stir an avoidable backlash. Promote media literacy and verification skills to identify misinformation and biased claims made that polarize public discourse. We must parent beyond emotional protectionism toward raising conscientious digital citizens.

Fostering Balance and Moderation

We have not suddenly ceased needing human intimacy, nature, silence, stories, and meaning. Yet we allow digital noise to deplete life's music as if virtual water might somehow quench the thirst for actual relationships. Demonstrate tuning technology out yourself to model presence. Turn phones face down to prevent the constant pull of notifications. Delete apps stealing attention impulsively all day without conscious choice. Read books, play board games, and ask engaging questions to enjoy shared family time technology-free. Set expectations around keeping tech usage in the proper perspective. It should never limit stillness, sleep, real connections, being fully engaged in academic lessons, or direct experiences happening right in front of us. Provide creative interests like learning instruments hands-on to prevent boredom from defaulting to screens readily. Guide children in discovering depth again through the people and passions that technology promises yet often displaces from our hurried lives when given the precedence it rarely deserves. Help reclaim what commitment to virtual visibility replaces if we fail to mindfully discern.

Also, commit to consistently enforcing media rules and limits, not occasionally or just when convenient. Integrate tech-life balance habits into your regular family culture. When breaches occur, collaborate on remedies, reminding all that wisdom governing technology prevents addiction; it's not some moral indictment. We limit dose-dependent seductions from replacing what truly fulfills. Monitor usage to match developmental maturity, as impulse control remains a work in progress. Through ongoing dialogue and our guidance, children gain growing savvy in navigating the unavoidable digital terrain ahead as citizens shaping humanity's course thoughtfully together.

Apply It! Creating Our Family Media Use Contract

Let's collaboratively design a formal contract codifying our household rules and responsibilities around technology use. This builds awareness together through clarity, teamwork, and accountability.

Supplies Needed:

Paper, pens, markers

Instructions:

1. Gather and brainstorm your current and ideal policies regarding media usage—screen time limits, device curfews, etiquette expectations, balancing virtual life with real-world priorities, etc. What's working? What needs improvement?

2. Distill ideas into 3–5 concise household rules/values that everyone consents to uphold. Phrase positively (e.g., be present during family meals).

3. Outline specific expectations aligned with each value, like putting phones away in a basket during dinner.

4. Define respective responsibilities (e.g., parents will model compliance themselves).

5. List privileges or rewards for keeping this contract, like extra reading time.

6. Write out the agreement cleanly on official paper signed by all family members to represent commitment.

7. Place it visibly as a reminder and revisit/evolve as needed. Consider sharing with friends and teachers, too, for motivation and accountability!

This tangible exercise raises awareness and gives children input and oversight while building trusting partnerships around technology's healthiest role in our lives collectively. Keep fine-tuning and using it collaboratively as we learn together!

Case Study: Promoting Balance

The Chang family—including parents Michael and Wendy and their three children Emma (14), Caleb (12), and Zoe (8)—realized technology was seriously eroding attention, mental health, and family connections. Devices were increasingly used impulsively without limits as leisure default rather than for specific purposes with intentional outcomes in mind.

Children reflexively checked their phones every few minutes, distracted from homework while awaiting college acceptances, and grades suffered. Siblings played individual video games side by side for hours without interacting as they once did. Parents lacked the energy to enforce reasonable restrictions after demanding jobs. Family stress and arguments intensified over these digital domination issues.

Utilizing this chapter's tips, the Changs instituted new household media policies through an official family contract created collaboratively and signed by all. This codified changes like no phones during meals, automating shutdowns after 9 pm across devices, and budgeting two hours designated daily for recreational interactive gaming alternating with offline creative activities.

The new structured approach allowed the family to gain growing clarity around usage and managing hectic schedules. It also prompted self-monitoring, realizing just how much time got lost mindlessly scrolling feeds or watching shows back-to-back. The visibility kept usage accountable.

With these helpful boundaries in place alongside parents deliberately modeling focus on real-world presence themselves, the Chang children made promising shifts toward better work/life balance. Siblings played more board and outdoor games together. Parents and children noticed improved academics through lessened digital distractions during homework. The family connection felt restored during newly rediscovered shared meal chatter.

While ongoing refinements are needed, this case study illustrates how, even in high-achieving households, simple, consistent limits regarding technology combined with intentional modeling of moderation by parents can reclaim space for what matters most—nurturing the minds and relationships that no application can ever replace.

Case Study: Raising Conscious Digital Citizens

As psychologists, Priya and Ravi Patel remained vigilant about social media's impacts on mental health and relationships. Before permitting accounts for their son Neil, 14, and daughter Tabitha, 11, Priya and Ravi committed to coaching the children on safe digital citizenship per this chapter's advice.

They began by frankly discussing the online dangers of bullying, impulsive oversharing, predatory strangers, and depression fueled by comparisons. Priya shared her own early regrets about not having privacy-protected accounts, which led to career fallouts. She explained the permanence of posted content to illustrate that restraint protects futures. Ravi guided setting all profiles to private.

Next, they explored the responsibilities of ethical technology usage, not just personal security and self-interest. Ravi asked reflective questions about pausing before posting reactions online. He described crimes enacted through anonymity and dehumanization of groups when unchecked emotions erupt digitally. Priya suggested imagining impacts if roles got reversed during conflicts. She urged civility, even online.

Ravi also initiated critical analysis of newsfeeds and memes, prompting children to research sources and evidence behind claims made to determine credibility and catch polarization. He assigned compare/contrast papers about influencers' content, balancing entertainment flair with educational substance.

Additionally, Priya guided Neil and Tabitha through digital goal-setting worksheets she created, listing skills they wished to showcase positively through careful posting. The children described wanting to inspire peers toward community service awards they earned themselves.

While social platforms posed risks, especially regarding comparison anxiety and jealousy, even in intact families, the Patels' guidance toward conscientious technology usage provided Neil and Tabitha scaffolds to interact online safely with compassion. Their approach nurtured priorities beyond popularity measured through viral posts and "likes." Instead, higher purpose and ethical citizenship took root as foundational filters for navigating digital spaces.

Bonus: Cultivating Emotional Intelligence as a Family

Emotional intelligence involves the ability to identify, understand, and regulate our own feelings while demonstrating empathy, social awareness, and care in relationships with others. As parents, developing these competencies in ourselves allows us to model critical behaviors for our children to integrate, too. Emotional intelligence proves essential for nurturing positive communication, conflict resolution, stress management, and deep relationships. Focus on these skills alongside academic development, which relies profoundly on self-awareness and maturity.

The Power of Special Time

Carving out consistent one-on-one special time with each child fosters trust and understanding. Without distractions, children open up about layered aspects of their inner world often missed in hurried daily life. Make special time a priority. Regular bonding sparks honesty and mentoring conversations that are otherwise rare when daily life feels saturated. Even a short weekly walk elicits nested emotions. Prioritize this oasis amid chaos.

Reflection: How often do you connect intentionally with each child without multitasking? What activities might you engage in together during special times? How could you adapt priorities to ensure regular bonding opportunities? Are schedules overloaded currently? Can you relinquish certain commitments, freeing up bonding time? What conversations arise when fully present?

Action Steps:

- Schedule 1–2 days/times per week designated for special time with each child.

- Select locations conducive to talking, like going for walks.

- Identify possible activities appealing to your child's interests.

Creative Expression of Emotions

Beyond labeling feelings, explore creative metaphorical modes conveying emotional experiences. These outlets provide children with constructive means of processing complex moods. Creative reflection builds emotional intelligence, regulation capacity, and verbal articulation skills over time.

Attempt the Feelings Portrait activity below, translating emotions into art. Or use house décor representing inner states with green plants symbolizing flourishing joy or dark curtains conveying grief. Weave emotional learning across mediums.

Feelings Portrait Activity

Supplies Needed: Paint, markers, and canvas or paper
Instructions:

1. Reflect on a feeling you've had lately

2. What images come to mind symbolizing that emotion? What color, texture, and shapes capture this? Can you think of any visual metaphors like the weather?

3. On your canvas, paint or draw representations of your feelings, translating the emotional essence. Allow shapes and hues to emerge intuitively.

4. Below your artwork, label the feeling portrayed. Discuss your translation experience with your family. Did visual language reveal any new self-insights?

Through metaphorical feeling expression, children better grasp life's emotional contours beyond one-dimensional happy/sad duality. Varied outlets also build self-knowledge, healthy regulation ability, and confidence, conveying vulnerability over time.

Goal-Setting Builds Purpose

Beyond day-to-day demands, guide children in mapping longer-term life visions, kindling their spark. Outline dreams in key areas like education, careers, relationships, self-improvement, hobbies, and community service. Concretize commitment to personal growth while upholding family bonds persisting beneath temporary role fluctuation as independence increases.

Use the Life Visioning template below or create vision boards with pictures representing future hopes. Revisit and update these North Stars quarterly, tracking evolution through the years. Allow some fluidity but with accountability and nurturing diligence, too. Support children owning what they're becoming!

Life Visioning Template

My 1-year vision is:_____

My 3-year vision is:_____

My 5-year vision is:_____

The skills I'll need are:_____

My action steps include:_____

Potential obstacles might be:_____

My supports will be:_____

To stay motivated, I will:_____

This orientation toward visualized futures motivates present goals and behaviors. It builds an emotional vision rooted in purpose. By focusing children beyond immediate gratification toward their highest selves, you equip them to structure life adventures intentionally while upholding responsibility.

Conflict Resolution Toolkit

Disagreements inevitably arise despite best intentions. Guide children in managing interpersonal disappointments and disputes through reconciliation. The three simple steps below foster conflict resolution while deepening relationship capacities long term.

The ABC Method

A = Acknowledge hurt feelings compassionately

B = Bridge perspectives through open communication

C = Compromise by cooperating on fair solutions

Step A involves validating emotions without blame before problem-solving. Often, hurt occurs even without cruel intentions. Start by offering empathy. "I understand you felt embarrassed when she said that. I would have, too." This emotional validation defuses fight-or-flight reactivity, opening minds.

Step B bridges understanding between parties through vulnerability, expressing needs, and then reflective listening until all feel genuinely heard and considered. Find common ground.

Finally, Step C compromises collaboratively so everyone's requirements get supported, not just compliance by one side resentfully. "How can we both feel respected through shared solutions?" This negotiation builds unity.

Helping children apply this ABC method to disagreements with parents and peers fosters political and relational capacities lasting a lifetime. Weave creative visioning and conflict resolution together by discussing how to handle obstacles that arise while pursuing cherished dreams. Guide children handling difficulty and differences with emotional skillfulness!

The Growth Mindset Difference

Beyond behaviors, nurture growth mindsets confronting challenges with optimism, not helpless resignation due to limiting self-talk about inadequate fixed abilities. Children absorb our subtle cues. Model boldness, trying new skills despite wobbles. Show them that their brain strengthens with practice. Reinforce small wins. Have them reframe setbacks as feedback, furthering goals through adjustment. Guide children to feeling empowered tackling difficulty with flexible strategies, asking for help, and modifying timelines without self-blame. Inspire their daring greatly! The path matters more than perfection.

Cultivating Compassionate Perspective-Taking

Expand children's empathy through discussing diverse experiences, volunteering together, role-playing social scenarios, and analyzing books and films from others' viewpoints. Nurture both cognitive and emotional empathy. The first involves intellectually understanding different reactions based on background. The latter contains intuitively identifying with people's feelings as your own. Guide children to nurture both mental flexibility and heart-centered sensitivity. Foster equality over ethnocentrism. Promote inclusion through actions—play dates with special needs students or making meals in women's shelters. Model speaking up against injustice, too. Children integrate our subtle ethical modeling about human dignity and courageous care daily.

Mindfulness Practices

Incorporate mindfulness practices, reducing reactivity and building self-regulation capacities. Teach deep breathing with visualizations, yoga poses increasing body awareness, sensory immersion outdoors, and simple meditation of noticing thoughts nonjudgmentally and then refocusing on the present. Convey that brains balance like seas through stillness after rocking emotions. Schedule five-minute family breathing breaks amid the rush. Lead by doing yourself. Over time, such pauses prevent small upsets from swelling into storms through distanced equanimity. Children embody our steadiness.

The Power of Family Meetings

Regular family meetings allow all members to share joys, concerns, and suggestions openly so needs get voiced, not buried. Gather consistently, not just when addressing crises. Foster democracy, including children in decision-making as appropriate. Maintain flexibility also—make space for renegotiating rules or schedules that prove unreasonable. Value transparency, compassion, and accountability, holding all generations to ethical standards. Demonstrate reconciling respectfully after inevitable conflicts, too.

Ensuring Productive Family Meetings

Designate a consistent weekly time without distractions. Have each member take turns facilitating using an agenda prepared in advance for focused progress. Begin appreciating family efforts noticed before raising new issues. Discuss challenges solving collaboratively. Conclude by acknowledging growth through even subtle unity gains made.

Family Meeting Conversation Starters:

- How did we spread kindness this week at home and in public?

- What expectations feel unreasonable to renegotiate presently?

- How can we bond more through meaningful activities together?

Family Meeting Checklist

Use the checklist below to ensure rich dialogue:
- Schedule meetings weekly at first, then monthly.

- Take turns facilitating the discussion.

- Start meetings appreciating family members' efforts.

- Discuss new needs and brainstorm possible solutions.

- Reevaluate previous expectations collaboratively.

- Share activity ideas, strengthening family fun and bonding.

- Conclude by hugging away any lingering tensions quickly.

This consistent relational forum reduces resentment through proactive input and keeps caregiving bonded to those impacted. Meet frequently and meet together!

Reflecting on Our Family Emotional Environment

What aspects of emotional intelligence building are you already modeling consistently without realizing it? How might you improve empathy, optimism, or conflict resolution abilities? Are patience, acceptance of uncomfortable feelings, responsible decision-making, and stress resilience displayed in balanced measures? How well are family meetings or collaborative goal setting already incorporated, and how might their impact grow? If each child felt safe grading your emotional leadership sincerely, what feedback might they share? What perceptual gaps do you need to fill?

Goal-Setting

for Family Emotional Health

What specific emotional intelligence goals would you like to achieve over the next year regarding mindfulness habits, family meeting implementation, improving parent/child trust and communication, etc.? Exactly how will you act to accomplish these aims? Who can support you when motivation dips? Outline your vision and responsibility plan here:

Our family vision for emotional growth:_____

Key skills we will build are:_____

Our action steps include:_____

To stay committed, we will:_____

In closing, remember that emotional health relies on patient nurturance over the years through modeling vulnerability, consistent dialogue, and unconditional support. Children thrive when encouraged, envisioning purposeful futures mattering beyond status or trends. Our steadiness through storms demonstrates that challenges can be handled with compassion. Keep sowing seeds of empathy and wisdom—in due time, vibrant fruits will grow. Remember that connectivity and understanding deepen gradually through consistency in meeting children where they stand developmentally today. Start small by instituting regular check-ins, creative sharing of feelings, or collaborative conflict resolution. Over time, these intentions fuse into intuitive habits, strengthening relationships to withstand greater storms ahead. Model humility and compassion toward yourself and loved ones throughout the process. For the goal remains not perfection but sustained nurturance, validating struggles and victories alike. Our steady presence conveys the message that through life's ups and downs, we remain in this together, progressing with wisdom and care. If we lead by valuing growth over glory, our children absorb emotional intelligence foundations that carry them resiliently forward.

Conclusion

In closing, let's recap core lessons from our exploration of nurturing children's social-emotional growth. While numerous strategies exist, certain best practices provide helpful through lines. As with any skill, parenting improves through a commitment to life-long learning and self-improvement.

Attune First, Guide Second

Before employing parenting techniques, focus first on emotional attunement and genuinely understanding your child's inner world. Listen without judging or problem-solving initially. Ensure that they feel safe to express tender feelings openly. When children feel heard and secure, they become more receptive to guidance moving forward. Remember, compassionate listening must come first. Start by offering children patient listening and a safe space to work through their own emotions before trying to direct or correct them.

As parents, it's easy to crave quick fixes when children struggle with challenges like bullying or loss. However, their greatest gift is our presence—sitting beside them through pain, not rushing to solve problems outright but instead ensuring emotional safety to unpack distress freely. This space allows inner wisdom to surface, guiding them toward renewed purpose. Raw vulnerability requires receptive ears and revolutionary patience standing witness without expectation.

Before layering on well-intended advice, first, emotionally attune. When confusion or despair strikes young hearts, suppress the urge to lecture adaptive techniques too fast. Simply listen, cradling their sensitivity within unconditional love. In time, growth unfolds organically if roots rest undisturbed. Your gentle mirroring will give them the space in which to self-validate amidst life's storms.

Communication Transforms Relationships

Consistently nurture positive communication habits, which profoundly impact family connections long-term. Speak using empathetic "I" statements over blame. Ask curious questions to understand meanings before reacting. Coach children through conflict using active listening. Model owning perspectives and apologizing for mistakes. Directives alone rarely reach hearts if delivered without care, attention, and vulnerability. Our words—and our receptive presence—possess the power to validate children, whether two years old or sixteen. The communication patterns we establish can either forge trust and understanding or inflict lasting emotional distance between parents and children.

Skilled communication seems simple yet requires much depth and delicacy. It's about authenticity—meeting your child's heart before their behavior. Ask, "What's really happening beneath the surface when you act this way?" Listen fully, suspending quick reactions. Help them name complex emotions, then guide processing constructively.

Speak with humility, too. Demonstrate taking responsibility when you inadvertently hurt them. "I apologize for dismissing your feelings earlier. Help me understand better." Model reconciliation repeatedly—this fosters emotional safety to raise issues openly, preventing distance.

Parenting communications can either bridge or break connections. But with conscientious nurturing of dialogue habits, children integrate skills for bravely engaging tensions in relationships throughout life with wisdom. Thus our leading by example becomes their instinctive blueprints carrying them forward.

Infuse Creativity

Into

Parenting

Given the repetitive duties of parenting, injecting creative playfulness sustains energy and connection over the long haul. Surprise children by turning chores into obstacle courses. Help shy children express emotions through journals displayed proudly. Take occasional breaks from rigid study schedules to stargaze. Find ways to laugh and be silly together between tears or discipline. Creativity reminds frazzled parents that mundane moments often hide unutilized opportunities to meaningfully engage. Infuse lightness and fun into parenting wherever possible to nourish the soul amidst the constant demands.

Parenting often feels dominated by problem-solving, household maintenance, and coordinating hectic schedules. Don't overlook the power of play! Injecting creative connections allows strained relationships to loosen— bellies aching with laughter, trading jokes, and hugging away headaches from constant school or career demands. Introduce hide and seek into chore routines. Request painted portraits capturing personality quirks you adore. Share poetry revealing whimsical dreams together.

Creativity sustains passion for parenting when doldrums inevitably hit. Inspire adventure by embroidering family history onto quilts. Compose songs gifting encouragement. Design games teaching life lessons playfully. When happiness feels in short supply, invent reasons for joy! Your inspiration reassures children that hard seasons pass. Delight lifts when we unveil imagination's wonder, never expiring if we persist in finding the light.

Focus on Progress Over Perfection

Acknowledge children's maturation as an incremental journey, not a linear race to some finish line. Provide patient guidance tailored to their developmental level—structure without rigidity, freedom without negligence. Meet them where they stand, then support their next reaches that move slightly beyond their current capabilities focused on growth, not grades. Moral habits like responsible technology usage require gradual reinforcement over years through models, not lectures. Nurture steady improvement until values stabilize intrinsically. Avoid rigid perfectionism about parenting or children, which crushes motivation.

Children aren't born wise. Emotional intelligence and character develop slowly through trial and error. Expect regression, like toddlers returning to crawling. Guide their ethical muscles to strengthen gradually through modeling, not mandates. Narrate small wins until goodness feels intrinsic.

Avoid comparing children's timelines either. Growth looks different for each child based on temperament and experiences. Your flexible support must match. Adapt higher expectations as new skills cement, backed by empathy when efforts fall short. Progress manifests through patience, not demanding perfect performance as the only praiseworthy outcome. Customize your approach based on the child you know, not society's standards.

Meet them where they are developmentally, then model virtues like courage and justice slightly ahead, inspiring their reach upward. With compassion, their ideal selves activate.

Parent With Purpose, Not Just Practicality

While parenting strategies provide helpful frameworks, stay grounded in overarching character development purposes beyond compliance. Why have rules if not for greater security to thrive? Why have consequences unless they are aligned with values? Our goal is not to indict children's core nature but to reveal their inner nobility. Explaining the rationale behind expectations builds self-discipline rooted in purpose. Help children understand the meaning behind requests instead of just expecting obedience.

Parenting cannot simply churn out compliant robots programmed to obey by repetition. It requires awakening human beings aware of greater whys animating actions. When directing children, explain higher aims, so they grow in wisdom. Rules exist to teach safety and respect. Chores assign responsibility, not punishment. Model interconnectedness.

Also, appeal to children's noble instincts by noting their positive impacts on others. "When you help Grandma, her difficult days feel happier." This intrinsic pride compounds over time more than obedience rewarding mere transactions. Inspire the generation's consciousness, elevating from unconsciousness.

Guide with a vision—how will your family's legacy uplift the community and humanity? Consider the parents your children's children urgently require. Then model those awakening virtues daily.

This process includes frustration and course corrections. Proceed with compassion—both for our children and ourselves—recalling that each represents a package of endless potential. Sealants now protect once wobbly legs. Smile at the small growth evident over time. For though seasons change, unconditional love alone cradles the promise within every generation to guide this world closer toward justice if we model ascending footpaths before them. Onward, we walk together. Stay patient with yourself and your children as you traverse this winding but meaningful path of growth side-by-side.

Final Case Study: The Wilson Family's Journey: Modeling Emotional Growth

When the Wilson twins Zoe and Kai were born, their parents, Angela and Jordan, felt overwhelmed but committed to nurturing their children's social-emotional health alongside meeting physical needs. However, the demands of newborn twins combined with financial strains meant Angela and Jordan struggled to find quality time with each baby. They often felt depleted, reacting harshly when the toddlers acted out for attention.

Angela began noticing signs of distress in anxious Zoe and aggressive Kai as the siblings reached elementary school age. Their pediatrician suggested getting support before behavioral issues escalated further. Angela and Jordan read books on parenting, prioritizing emotional connection even when exhausted.

Angela made a point of scheduling weekly one-on-one dates with each twin focused on listening versus problem-solving nonstop. Kai opened up about classmates teasing his stuttering. Angela provided empathy, not dismissal, naming the sadness and frustration he felt. She shared stories of her own childhood shyness to nurture trust. Meanwhile, Jordan initiated collaborative art projects with Zoe on weekends when she seemed most overwhelmed by responsibilities. Their creativity released anxiety to voice dreams.

When the pandemic hit months later, Angela held ongoing family meetings to encourage sharing feelings about isolation and grief over lost social opportunities. She became deliberate about expressing her own emotions transparently to model healthy processing. The consistent safe space to unpack distress prevented dysfunctional coping behaviors from taking root within the twins.

As the twins matured through early adolescence, Angela actively reinforced the emotional intelligence skills she wished to impart. She prompted journaling to nurture self-awareness, coached them through anxiety using mindfulness techniques, and facilitated resolutions after fights about who gets the next turn on the video game console. Jordan also guided goal-setting, encouraging the twins to outline future dreams beyond just reacting day-to-day. He reminded them of their strengths and potential regularly.

Now, as high schoolers, though still benefiting from empathetic support, the twins display promising resilience, self-confidence, and relationship skills cultivated through their parents' conscious commitment to emotional nurturance—even when past exhaustion or upset made patience difficult. Kai advocates for disability rights within school leadership. Zoe fuels her community volunteer work by writing inspiring poetry. Looking back, they both express gratitude for their parents' devotion through the years to nurturing communication, security, and unconditional love as foundations enabling them to find purpose and shine bright.

The Wilson family's journey conveys how parents can interrupt dysfunctional generational cycles by choosing emotional attunement first, even when time and energy feel limited. Their mindful effort focusing on consistent listening, expressive encouragement, and compassionate modeling planted seeds yielding remarkable personal growth over time. Despite ongoing mistakes and learning, Angela and Jordan's dedication nurtured the twins' social-emotional health beautifully, prioritizing connection that now ripples outward through engaged, purposeful young adults embracing their full potential.

The Anand Family: Fostering Empathy and Responsibility

From the outset of parenting, Priya and Raj Anand were committed to nurturing ethical responsibility and empathy alongside academic achievements for their gifted son Neil and passionate daughter Tabitha. However, the parents often felt depleted trying to balance the professional demands of their counseling careers with present family connections. They recognized a disconnect between teaching emotional intelligence theoretically at work versus practicing inclusivity and attunement consistently at home. Even as licensed therapists, they found it challenging to embody the social-emotional nurturance they encouraged clients to provide children. Their own fatigue often obscured modeling patient listening and unconditional love. Priya and Raj had to acknowledge the gaps between their aspirations and their impact.

When a teacher contacted Priya about Neil's lack of focus during lessons, she reflected on the misalignment between their family intentions and impact. She and Raj assessed the need to model the self-care and stress management they encouraged clients to practice. They began taking mini-mindfulness breaks together before dinnertimes rather than researching cases. They made space for both children to express extracurricular interests instead of overloading busy schedules. Priya and Raj recognized that achieving professional success meant nothing if their children felt neglected emotionally. It was time to walk their talk even amidst exhaustion.

As their family rhythms realigned with more margin for bonding, Priya also became deliberate about nurturing cooperative play between the two versus excessive solo activities. She reinforced praising their generosity when Neil comforted Tabitha over a failed piano recital, and Tabitha showed Neil her latest violin composition. Priya highlighted the deeper connections music forged between them. Priya realized that, just as with clients, verbal encouragement when her children displayed empathy nurtured those traits in the long term. She had to notice and voice awe over kindnesses.

When technology exacerbated attention span challenges a few years later, the Anands held collaborative family meetings to institute household media limits, improving sleep, productivity, and real-world socializing. They forfeited personal device usage to demonstrate balance. The new board game nights and bike rides cemented unity away from fracturing screens. Priya remembered from counseling experience that children model behaviors seen not rules dictated. Raj and Priya had to exemplify media moderation first.

Now, as teens, Neil mentors immigrant students needing ESL support by drawing on his own heritage. Tabitha cofounded an arts enrichment program for children lacking creative outlets when families endure financial hardships. Despite unrelenting societal pressures and competition, the Anand children learned to ground identity in compassionate character above achievements or appearances. The seeds of empathy bore sweet fruit in young adulthood through the Anands' conscious commitment, nurturing cultural consciousness and courage early on.

While their parenting journey continues needing occasional course corrections, Priya and Raj modeled resonantly that no external success replaces nurturing intrinsic humanity within families first. This consistent emotional attunement and ethical centering seeded community-focused young adults glowing gently from the inside out. The Anands' humility in committing to personal growth as lifelong learners ultimately guides the next generation to pay forward the gifts they themselves received. Though still learning, the Anands exemplified sustainability, shifting priorities toward presence using self-honesty and wisdom.

References

Bond, L., Carlin, J. B., Thomas, L., Rubin, K., & Patton, G. (2001). Does bullying cause emotional problems? A prospective study of young teenagers. *BMJ*, *323*(7311), 480–484. https://doi.org/10.1136/bmj.323.7311.480

Gottman, J. (2011). *Raising An Emotionally Intelligent Child*. Simon and Schuster.

Mattingly, L. (2021). *Love Yourself*. Rockridge Press.

Seligman, M. E. P., & Csikszentmihalyi, M. (2000). Positive psychology: An introduction. *American Psychologist*, *55*(1), 5–14. https://doi.org/10.1037/0003-066x.55.1.5

Stein, S., & Book, H. E. (2011). *The EQ Edge: emotional intelligence and your success*. Jossey-Bass.

Printed in Great Britain
by Amazon